ATTRACTING HUMMINGBIRDS

HOW TO DESIGN BACKYARD ENVIRONMENTS USING FEEDERS AND FLOWERS

DANIEL I STEIN

RMC PUBLISHERS

© Copyright 2021 - All rights reserved.

It is not legal to reproduce, duplicate, or transmit any part of this document in either electronic means or in printed format. Recording of this publication is strictly prohibited and any storage of this document is not allowed unless with written permission from the publisher except for the use of brief quotations in a book review.

TABLE OF CONTENTS

Introduction	v

PART I: FLIGHTS
1. WINTER HOLIDAYS	5
2. HEADING NORTH	9
3. MATING SEASON	25
4. NESTING	37
5. RAISING A FAMILY	45
6. RETURNING SOUTH	55

PART II: FEEDERS
7. CHOOSING YOUR FEEDER	67
8. PLACING YOUR FEEDER	77
9. WINDOW COLLISIONS	81
10. PREPARING THE NECTAR	87
11. CLEANING & MAINTENANCE	91
12. COMMON PROBLEMS & SOLUTIONS	95

PART III: FLOWERS
13. DESIGNING YOUR GARDEN	105
14. THE FOUR ESSENTIALS	109
15. PLANT SELECTION	117
16. MAINTENANCE & SAFETY	123
17. RISKS TO HUMMINGBIRDS	129
18. PHOTOGRAPHY QUICK GUIDE	135

CONCLUSION	139
NORTH AMERICAN HUMMINGBIRD SPECIES	143
Allen's Hummingbird	145
Anna's Hummingbird	146
Antillean Crested Hummingbird	147

Bahama Woodstar	148
Berylline Hummingbird	149
Black-Chinned Hummingbird	150
Blue-Throated Mountain-Gem	151
Broad-Billed Hummingbird	152
Broad-Tailed Hummingbird	153
Buff-Bellied Hummingbird	154
Cinnamon Hummingbird	155
Calliope Hummingbird	156
Costa's Hummingbird	157
Cuban Emerald	158
Green-Breasted Mango	159
Green Violet-Ear Hummingbird	160
Lucifer Sheartail	161
Plain Capped Star-Throat	162
Rivoli's Hummingbird	163
Ruby-Throated Hummingbird	164
Rufous Hummingbird	165
Violet-Crowned Hummingbird	166
White-Eared Hummingbird	167
Xantus Hummingbird	168
Image Credits	169
Endnotes	179

INTRODUCTION

Wherever you look, nature is telling stories.

Some have been known to us since ancient times, while others have yet to be discovered. But not all of nature's stories manage to resonate with us the same way. Instead, we seem to have an almost magnetic attraction to seek out the most extreme stories in the world around us.

This innate urge to know the limits of what is possible pulls us the strongest when exploring the animal kingdom. The severe and brutal trade-offs needed to specialize into the tiniest ecological niches create the strangest and most beautiful animals, with the most exciting and dangerous lives, and of course, the best stories.

If someone were to ask: what is the fastest animal? The tallest? The largest? The oldest?

Several answers, or at least strong possibilities, probably spring immediately to mind, along with an innate understanding of the narrative of those lives. What compromises were made in their bodies and behavior to be the best at what they do: did they trade strength for speed, do they endure fragility for access to unreachable food, or have they increased in size for safety and security? The animal kingdom's best-known stories are also reflected in our own, through the sacrifices made by the most successful, creative, and driven people.

But despite our attraction and connection to these extremes of nature, we rarely have the opportunity to witness them in person. Usually, the limits of nature are far away in the untamed and inaccessible wilderness, only visible through a screen, imagined on the pages of a book, or viewed as a tamed replica in a zoo.

However, there is a notable exception – hummingbirds. These are the smallest birds, with the fastest wings and the longest migrations (relative to size), and that merely scratches the surface of their incredible lives. Every part of a hummingbird's body, behavior, and battle for survival is unique. And hummingbirds don't live in a far-off jungle, the ocean depths, or a precarious mountaintop. Instead, they live right on our doorsteps.

And not only do they share our backyards, but a symbiotic relationship has been established between humans and hummingbirds. Hummingbirds provide us a window into the wild and a convenient connection to it. At the same time, we can readily offer them food, shelter, and security. While this agreement might seem reminiscent of a domesticated house cat or loyal dog, hummingbirds remain wild creatures and need to be treated as such.

Attracting hummingbirds to your backyard so that you can fully appreciate their story is only the beginning. Hummingbirds pique our interest and entertain us for hours, yet most of us are not aware of the intimate details of their lives, the intricacies of their behaviors, or the vastness of their species. As with any specialist in nature, they have many complex behavior patterns and needs. This book will help you recognize these patterns and give you the tools to create healthy habitats for them.

If you just can't wait to set-up feeders in your backyard or on your balcony (Part 2), or feel the need to immediately begin designing your hummingbird garden for next spring (Part 3), please feel free to skip ahead. Just remember to come back and discover more about your newfound friends in Part 1, so that you can fully appreciate these miniature marvels.

Helping hand — Anna's hummingbird recovering from a fall on Vancouver Island

Hummingbird Basics

There are approximately 361 species of hummingbird – more than any other type of bird – all living in the Americas. However, the exact number is a matter of debate, as some organizations recognize subspecies as independent species of their own. As a result, you might see different numbers of hummingbird species in various sources.

Hummingbirds are found only in the New World region and are, in fact, banned from Hawaii![1] They also have the honor of being the smallest migratory bird, with the bee hummingbird of Cuba being the smallest of any bird species. At the same time, some hummingbirds have incredibly long migratory journeys to make. That alone is amazing, given that a hummingbird's metabolism requires them to feed every few hours to survive.

INTRODUCTION

The variety of hummingbird species is staggering, as is the range of their sizes. The bee hummingbird mentioned earlier weighs a scant 1.6 grams, about the same as a jumbo-sized paperclip, and measures only two inches (five cm) from beak to tail.

In contrast, the largest hummingbird, the aptly named giant hummingbird of the South American Andes, is over twelve times heavier, weighing in at 20 grams, and is 9.1 inches (23 cm) long. The bee hummingbird buzzes around, flapping its wings 80 times a second or more in a blur that seems unreal and creates the hummingbird's signature sound. While the giant hummingbird flaps away at a leisurely ten beats per second – almost slowly enough to be observed.

Along with these differences in size and scale, hummingbird species have a wide variety of distinguishing characteristics, and it's not just the more colorful males that are unique. While the tropical South American species tend to have more exaggerated features, many North American species have vibrant, iridescent feathers, elaborate head crests, and specialized tails or bills that can make them instantly recognizable.

Hummingbirds are often named after their most unique feature or their dominant color, and most hummingbird names use a color along with a term identifying the location of that distinguishing feature, like emerald-bellied, white-tailed, violet-eared, indigo-capped, and black-throated. It may be tricky at first, but with a little bit of practice, anyone can learn the names and appearances of the most common hummingbirds in their area.

Unique features — left: sword-billed, top right: snowcap, bottom right: swallow-tail

Yet what we see in our gardens or at feeders is only a fraction of the complex life of hummingbirds. Their diet, behavior, and adaptability to the demands of a changing environment are hidden behind a curtain of wilderness. So much of the lives of hummingbirds are unknown to most of us, because they live a relatively secret existence and almost always a solitary one.

We can surmise what transpires out of sight. Still, only the most dedicated ornithologists have scraped together detailed data on these birds of the Americas. The marvel is not their flying ability, but their ability to survive from Tierra del Fuego to Alaska, from the Maritimes of Eastern Canada to the deserts of Arizona and the Pacific coast.

Charles Darwin could only dream of exploring the evolution of this adaptable animal.

HUMMINGBIRDS AND HUMANS

Hummingbirds are a symbol of summer and convey many different meanings for North and South American cultures. For example, some people believe that hummingbirds can be spiritual conduits and that if a hummingbird lands on you, it signifies that a deceased friend or relative is trying to contact you.

The Mayans believed that the hummingbird was the sun in disguise, descended to earth to court the moon. Mexicans have a myth about a Tarascan Indian woman, taught the art of beautiful basket making by hummingbirds who had woven their own beautiful nests. The Aztec god Huitzilopochtli ("hummingbird of the south") was a sun god and god of war. Aztecs believed that when warriors died, they transformed into hummingbirds so they could fly and join this god. The Taino people of Columbia saw hummingbirds as representing rebirth and they were considered symbolic of peace and protection; yet, at the same time, the Taino warriors were called the Hummingbird Warriors. There is a parallel between the aggressive Taino warriors and their history of taking over new territory, and the male hummingbird rushing ahead to the breeding grounds to take over his chosen territory.

In North American Indigenous cultures, hummingbirds represent harmony and industriousness and are seen as healers who help people in need. For some, hummingbirds are seen as bringers of good luck and love, represented by the symbol of infinity in the pattern of the hummingbird's rapidly beating wings. The Métis of Manitoba and

Saskatchewan have, in turn, adopted the infinity symbol as their flag.

Much of the mystique surrounding hummingbirds extends even to their common names. The buff-belly, the calliope, and Rivoli's hummingbird may seem relatively exotic but innocuous. However, names like lucifer and the Jamaican mango are peculiar, especially since mangoes do not grow in Jamaica. Fiery topaz, hook-billed hermit, hyacinth visor-bearer, and shining sunbeam add to the long list of exotic names, along with flying jewel, purple-crowned fairy, glittering-throated emerald, peacock coquette, and sapphire-vented puff-leg.

Yet their playful exotic names seem to fit them perfectly. And who could argue against the reality that they make each of us feel immensely better as we observe them in our yards?

In probing the hummingbird mystique, we embrace the qualities that we humans most admire: dedication and perseverance, beauty and agility, grace and dexterity. While we might feel envious of any person embodying all of these qualities, the more familiar we become with our tiny, humming neighbors, and the more we compare their habits and behaviors to ours, the more we are endeared to them. Familiarity fosters love and respect.

It is with this love and a passion for understanding the wild world around us that I have written this book. I hope to strengthen our emotional connection to the hummingbird with information that makes our reality seem even more fantastic than our imagination.

The best stories need details before they can come alive and connect with us.

In Part 1, we'll follow a couple of our North American hummingbird friends on a year-long journey, occasionally looking in on some of their South and Central American relatives. From their winter vacations in the southern USA and Central America, their journey takes them northward, back to the place of their birth, through the summer feeding and breeding frenzies in Canada and the continental USA, before they return south for winter. We will immerse ourselves in their lives and sneak into their secret world.

PART I: FLIGHTS

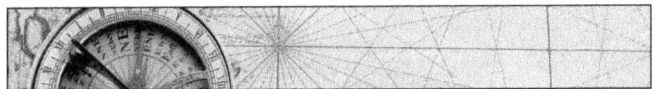

Two species will provide sufficient information to lure us into embracing the hummingbird enthusiastically: the rufous and the ruby-throated hummingbird. As two of the most commonly encountered species, the rufous and ruby have territories that cover enough of the North American continent between them to represent their entire family. These two species will paint a picture of how and why hummingbirds thrive.

Any good biography begins with a bit of family history and background information. Both rufous and ruby have great stories to start us off with. The two species are dramatically different in temperament, behavior, and lifestyle.

Rufous is a rough-and-ready wilderness survivalist named for its bronze-brown colors. It is promiscuous, driven, pushy, aggressive, and honestly, somewhat of a jerk. Rufous hummingbirds live to fight, and will attempt to dominate any other birds that approach their territory regardless of their size. They have been known to attack larger animals, predators, songbirds, and even crows or ravens to protect their mating or feeding area. You can easily remember the personality of Rufous as it sounds similar to "rough house". It is a little fireplug.

Rufous is a west coast resident with a range that runs from California and western Mexico all the way north to Alaska. Upper range estimates of the rufous population reach up to 19 million[1]. However, the rufous is one of the more at-risk species in North America. Only recently has it begun to expand eastward across the Rocky Mountains into the prairies. Nevertheless, it remains the dominant species in this range.

Rufous hummingbird — left: male, right: female

Ruby is more laid back. Considered by many to be more attractive and appealing, Rubies have a somewhat more leisurely lifestyle. Ruby-throated hummingbirds tend to prefer the suburban, slower pace of life, drifting between feeders and relaxing more often. They are the dancers of the hummingbird world in North America, often diving 50 feet or more in courtship dives, appearing fragile yet remaining resilient.

Ruby-throated hummingbirds are the most widely-ranging species in North America. With a territory that extends from the southern USA and northern Mexico, eastward to the east coast of the USA and the Maritimes in Canada, and swoops westward through Ontario to central Canada. A small finger of their 34-million-strong population[2] extends almost to the Rockies and brushes up against rufous territory.

Ruby-throated hummingbird — left: male, right: female

1
WINTER HOLIDAYS

Seasons for hummingbirds are broken into four roughly equal segments: winter holidays, northern migration, breeding season, and southern migration.

While hummingbirds are the smallest migrating bird, all migrating hummingbirds follow a similar winter routine: the males and females winter in separate regions, feed casually on abundant flowers and insects, and, like humans on a tropical getaway, they loaf around for up to three months.

While we won't stay with the South American relatives of rufous and ruby for long, they do demonstrate some of the more interesting adaptations of hummingbirds.

For example, hummingbird bills vary between species and they are adapted to the food source that is most prevalent in a given habitat. The bills are surprisingly soft, and protect the hummingbirds' long tongues, while forming a seal to allow them to collect nectar. In South America, the sword-billed hummingbird has a beak that is over half its eight-inch (20 cm) length, adapted over thousands of years to reach into very long-necked flowers of the mid to high Andes, such as the sacred flower of Venezuela, the cantuta. Other species, such as the lucifer hummingbird and sickle-billed hummingbird, have curved bills that allow them exclusive access into specialized flowers while hovering.

It often isn't clear to scientists which came first, the changes to bill shape or the evolution of more complex tubular flowers, and over time both have changed with each other. In some species, even the males and females may have different shaped bills. The males may compete for common flowers with high nectar content, while the females rely on a separate, scarcer food source that can only be reached with a longer or more drastically curved bill.

However, recently it has been proposed that some male hummingbirds have evolved straighter, more rigid bills to better engage in aerial combat[1]. Additional weaponry, like points, hooks, or teeth on their bills can make males more fearsome competitors and better able to defend territory, but make feeding more difficult.

 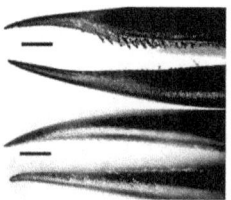

Tough customer — left: tooth-billed hummingbird, right: close-up of male (top) and female (bottom) bills with and without 'teeth'

Over ninety percent of hummingbirds do not migrate, and these 335 or so species stay in their comfortable tropical homes in Latin America. So, before we fully dive into the lives of the rufous and ruby, we should ask why it is that some species risk everything on annual marathons across the Americas. The exact stimulus and reason for hummingbird migration are only speculated upon.

The competition for food does not adequately explain the drive to migrate in some but not others. The changing seasons or angle of the sun do not trigger a migration response in every species. And thousands of other bird species, from songbirds to birds of prey, do not migrate while their cousins do. It is a Darwinian dilemma that is not fully understood.

One theory is that the few members of the hummingbird family that migrate do so because the competition for food in the jungles of southern Mexico and Panama is intense. Yet, millions of birds remain year-round without the threat of starvation.

Another theory is that the changes in daylight hours trigger an urge to migrate. While this may be true in the north as summer comes to a close, between the tropical belts of Cancer and Capricorn, where most hummingbirds spend winter, daylight hours remain almost constant.

Perhaps early hummingbirds began migrating after the Ice Age, and discovered easy access to food sources as the summer season emerged and spread northward. This expansion is similar to how humans spread out and populated the world, beginning in eastern Africa. It is also similar to how jellyfish have settled the east coast of North America as those waters have warmed.

Or maybe earlier relatives were carried astray on the winds that often blow southwest to northeast across Mexico. This accident of weather seems consistent with the dense populations of ruby-throated hummingbirds in the eastern USA and Canada.

Perhaps ancient hummingbirds were forced out of their territories by more dominant relatives, compelling them to find new food sources and nesting areas. It is not uncommon with other birds to see a few pioneers arrive in an area before the main onslaught.

This theory also seems promising. There are currently three species of tropical hummingbirds, formerly found only in the Caribbean islands, that can now be found in Florida. Similarly, two species native to south Central America can now be found in the southwest USA.

Regardless of why the migration is made, after a languid winter, the hectic schedules of the following three seasons are a stark contrast.

2

HEADING NORTH

Hummingbirds travel alone, much the same way they live. While hummingbirds may seem gregarious and social toward us, they rank as some of the most solitary animals in the world.

Many other birds who separate during the migration and breeding seasons make an effort to congregate again as an extended family in the fall, including crows, blackbirds, and geese. Even monarch butterflies gather by the millions in central Mexico to conserve heat as they huddle together. Hummingbirds could benefit from this shared body warmth, too, but have not developed this behavior. Instead, hummingbirds strive to drive their family away in the summer. Even in their wintering grounds, hummingbirds do not congregate at all. There is nothing social in their migration flights, either.

A large flock of hummingbirds would not accomplish the defensive aim of most migratory flocking birds. A few dozen hummingbirds would seem like only a handful of larger birds to overhead predators. To travel in a flock might actually increase the danger for the hummingbird.

The aerodynamic advantages for larger birds to fly in patterns and save energy by riding in each other's slipstreams do not materialize here either, as hummingbirds' rapid wing movements and small size require them to create their own airflow.

And of course, if they flocked together, all would compete for that same meager supply when any one of them detected food.

Thus, they travel one at a time and only encounter each other infrequently.

Each year rufous, ruby, and another eighteen or so of their North and Central American cousins leave the comfort of the tropics and trek along their migratory routes. A few species make enormous trips, while others migrate only short distances.

The migration occurs on a predictable timetable, starting between the end of January to the middle of February for most species. Two species, Allen's and Costa's hummingbirds, can actually start migrating in December, but do not make the huge journeys of the rufous or ruby-throated hummingbirds.

The map at the end of this chapter reveals the progress that the two major North American species – rufous and ruby – make during the two-and-a-half to three-month trip. One thing that is certain with the migration timetable is that it coincides with the availability of food, since these delicate birds have such high metabolism that they must feed every few hours or die.

Therefore, preparation for migration is vital, in the same way that we humans prepare for an extended vacation – well, almost the same way.

Hummingbirds, both on their northern journey and their return trip south for the winter, feed voraciously for the few weeks prior to departure. It may be hard to think of a 2–6 gram bird 'putting on weight' and 'getting fat', but they will gain as much as twenty-five percent of their body weight in those weeks before heading north, then up to fifty percent of their body weight before returning south. These fat reserves will be almost entirely consumed during their travels. On the other hand, humans tend to struggle to remove the excess weight they gain on a holiday.

The rufous migrates from central and southern Mexico to southern Alaska, while the ruby-throated hummingbird has an almost equally daunting migration, from the Yucatán Peninsula in southern Mexico, along the entire Eastern Seaboard of the USA and Canada, and as far north as the middle of the Canadian prairies.

Rufous begins its journey from the west coast of Mexico, with some individuals traveling an entire 3,600 miles (6,000 kilometers) to reach Alaska, hugging the western mountain ranges of the Pacific. The rufous completes the entire migration in 120 days, or 30 miles (50 kilometers) per day, while most common birds can only manage daily distances of 20 to 25 miles. The rufous migration distance is considered the longest bird migration relative to size. Even though ocean birds like the Arctic tern can trek up to

12,000 miles (19,000 kilometers) between the Arctic and Antarctic, they are much larger.

In the past century, the rufous has moved further north and slightly west, finding new food sources and more moderate climates. Because these birds tend to be more inclined to live in the wilderness, they are not tempted to make a home in urban areas like ruby-throated hummingbirds have done. Instead, they range further to find food as they are either pushed out of their natural habitat or seek new frontiers. However, they do tend to demonstrate a pioneering instinct.

For a bird that prefers a warm winter, rufous is somewhat more adaptable to the cold than most other species. They can tolerate temperatures that fall a little below the threshold of 20°F (-7°C) that is the lower limit for rubies and most other hummingbird species. That allows them to explore farther north.

Along its north route, the rufous comes into contact with several other west coast species. Anna's hummingbird is one of those. While Anna's may travel a few hundred miles to establish a feeding territory with the varying seasons, it does not truly migrate. However, Anna's range has expanded in recent decades. It can now be found all the way north to Vancouver Island and as far east as Arizona, and occasionally spends the winter in Canada. Many are now even spotted east of the Mississippi every fall and winter, crossing into the ruby's territory.

A similar species to the rufous, Allen's hummingbird is less intense in its migratory objectives and only makes it as far north as northern California. Still, it, too, is expanding its reach, with populations now found in western Arizona and Nevada, and a few even in Oregon.

Anna's hummingbird — left: male, right: female

Other species found along the west coast route in addition to the rufous, include the calliope and black-chinned hummingbirds.

Rufous is also not the only northern wanderer. Costa's hummingbirds, which are desert-dwellers, have been spotted as far north as Alaska, Alberta, and British Columbia. The broad-tailed hummingbird visits as far north as Montana to breed.

Rufous hummingbirds could be considered the 'traveling salesmen' of the hummingbird world. They are promiscuous, often wooing a few females at a time and breeding with several. However, they also show no discrimination, breeding with a variety of other hummingbird species that they meet along the way, like the Costa's, black-chinned, Anna's, Allen's, and lucifer hummingbirds. This behavior has led to a number of subspecies evolving along the west coast of North America. Yet, the rufous remains one of the most solitary of the hummingbirds, vigorously defending their right to privacy and living as far into the wilderness as they can.

In recent decades, some rufous hummingbirds have opted to overwinter as far north as British Columbia. The abundance of feeders and backyard gardens at which they willingly but sparingly feed provide them with sufficient food. At the same time, the changing climate has moderated coastal winter temperatures. Urban centers also trap heat for the birds. And perhaps a few are just tired of the journey!

West coast neighbors — top left: male Allen's hummingbird, top right: male black-chinned hummingbird, bottom left: male calliope hummingbird, bottom right: male broad-tailed hummingbird

HEADING NORTH

Meanwhile, leaving roughly the same time as the rufous departs from its wintering grounds, the ruby starts out.

The ruby migration starts at the end of January. The winds become more variable as warm weather seeks a foothold. These weather systems often give the ruby some assistance in the early stages of their migration, as winds tend to move west to east in the lower states during February and March. However, it is not uncommon to have severe storms blow out of the north by late March. Therefore, any late-traveling rubies will need to hunker down and wait for warmer weather. The stragglers will arrive in the last week of May or the first week of June.

The complete northern migration can last up to 134 days (19 weeks) or over a third of the year. Fortunately, few birds take this long to complete a half migration, and most rubies can finish their journey in about two-thirds of that time, about 13 weeks. The southbound return trip proceeds even more quickly, with northern and north-westerly winds assisting their travels.

Despite the perceived leisurely pace of the ruby migration and the much shorter distance compared to the rufous, it is one of nature's most impressive journeys.

On the first day of the male ruby-throated hummingbird's trip, he demonstrates a unique level of stamina and perseverance. He begins his journey by flying from the Yucatán peninsula in southeastern Mexico, across the 500-mile expanse of the Gulf of Mexico in one night.

The excursion begins at nightfall, and he will navigate the entire stretch over the Gulf without stopping for food. Often, the trip will continue into the next day. A few enterprising birds may stop briefly to rest on ships or oil rigs in the Gulf, but the crossing must be completed in about eighteen hours. A nasty headwind will doom most to failure. So not only must the male rubies gorge on food before departing, but they must also time their trip to avoid bad weather.

> *On average, a ruby beats its wings fifty times per second. On an eighteen-hour flight across the Gulf of Mexico, the ruby-throated hummingbird would, therefore, have to flap its wings over three million times.*

It is a precipitous gamble, since the weather in that region can change dramatically within hours. Tornado season in the south starts as early as late January and early February, exposing the rubies to even more hazardous conditions. Along the way, late winter ice and snowstorms are common. Since these birds rarely fly above eighty feet, the endurance of the rubies as they buck the winds and turbulence over the Gulf is astounding.

This is an excellent test of the male ruby's understated determination. The male, after all, sets out a couple of weeks before the female. It is a race for this sex, and crossing the Gulf is a huge shortcut. Each wants – or, more accurately, needs – to arrive early in his destination to claim and defend his chosen territory. Only the best territory, the best display of his male extravagance, will win the favor of a female ruby. But rushing comes with a price, as the males are on the cusp of the fragile, emerging food supply and risk encountering dangerous weather patterns as they travel.

A few weeks after the male rubies leave Mexico, the females set upon their own journeys. Like the males, they travel alone, feeding on nectar, bird feeders, sap, water, and insects. However, the insect population has risen since the males' departure, and flowers are now starting to bloom. The trip has become much less dangerous. Many females also opt to travel a more circuitous route, around the Gulf and over land. This delay ensures that the flowers and insects are emerging along their path, preparing them as they arrive for mating season.

It is unknown if the females, who judge a male on its ability to grab a great feeding territory, also consider an abundance of artificial bird feeders to qualify as a feeding site, but they do judge on the available flowers and insects.

This first wave of male ruby-throated hummingbirds follows, almost in lock-step, the migration northward of yellow-breasted sapsuckers. Outlier members of the woodpecker family, the sapsuckers also conduct a full migration each year. Likely neither the sapsucker nor hummingbird are aware of this shadowing, or of being shadowed, by the other, since they follow different migration rhythms. In addition, the hummingbirds only travel in the daytime (with the exception of that first overnight trip across the Gulf of Mexico), both because temperatures are warmer, and so they can spot food more readily, as hummingbird night vision is poor.

Female sapsuckers winter farther south than the males, often traveling to South or Central America for the winter. As a result, their northern migration tends to be closer to the migration timetable of the rubies. Still, both male and female sapsuckers open sap veins along the way, providing a helpful emergency food supply for the migrating rubies. The sap from new boreholes or scrapes provides the early-arriving male rubies with the energy they require to make the 2,000 mile (3,000+ km) journey from Mexico to Canada.

Hummingbirds rarely travel much above the treetops, even though a few have been spotted as high as five hundred feet. The open air above the trees leaves the small birds exposed to predators and vulnerable to the wind. Hummingbirds need to avoid traveling in contrary winds and storms to prevent them from being blown astray. Flying lower also gives them the opportunity to snag the small bugs and emerging insects on which they regularly feed. Finally, hummingbirds need to rest occasionally, and they can generally only travel short distances at a time. Traversing the route in shorter daily hops and stops breaks up the trip into more manageable pieces. Still, it exposes them to environmental risks like changing weather.

Even though hummingbirds can fly up to 25 mph (40 kph) in short bursts, they do not travel many hours each day. Their daily flight path is typically shorter than twenty-five miles, as they navigate near shelter where possible and feed every few hours. However, flying low in a serpentine path around vegetation and other obstacles, instead of above them, can result in those twenty-five miles of straight-line progress becoming double that in reality.

The sapsuckers also time their travel north based on weather conditions but fly longer distances each day than the hummingbird, also traveling just above the height of the trees.

The journey for both sexes of the ruby can start in southern Mexico, Belize, or even Nicaragua and Panama. Migration can also end at various points through the United States, the Maritimes, or any of the Canadian provinces east of British Columbia. Here, at their destination, they will breed. It is like snow drifting in a winter storm: little flakes and drifts of birds abandon the longest run of the migration to establish homes in a territory with which they are familiar.

Generally, rubies return very near to where they were born. In this way, they are already familiar with food sources, both natural and supplied by people.

As the rufous and ruby near their northern destinations, their daily journeys can slow a bit, as they run out of fat stores and have to wait for flowers to bloom. However, changing weather patterns in North America have meant that many flowers bloom earlier in parts of the continent and later in others. Disruptions wreak havoc for hummingbirds, who are compelled to follow their schedule almost to the day of their usual arrival.

While many of Canada's hummingbird species are extending their range, the rufous and ruby have expanded their territory the most. They are now raising families where they were not seen a few decades ago. Rufous is a pioneer in Alberta now, while ruby can be found in northern parts of Manitoba, the middle of Saskatchewan, and a large swath of Alberta. It is possible that, within a few more decades, the two will meet up somewhere in Alberta or British Columbia, or even southern Alaska.

At the same time, a couple of species from the Sierra Nevada range are spreading eastward into Arizona, and Anna's is reaching further north in British Columbia. All are finding abundant food and more favorable breeding, nesting, and feeding conditions.

So long as the hummingbird territorial expansion continues, it bodes well for the population, since these birds are expanding primarily because of the abundance of food rather than searching for dwindling resources. But as they migrate into what were formerly inhospitable regions, they risk being exposed to erratic weather conditions and unpredictable food supplies.

Fortunately, all hummingbirds can benefit from the awareness of humans along the route who place feeders out early and who plant vegetation that is an invitation to traveling or resident hummingbirds (more in Parts 2 and 3).

Currently, those birds that have always migrated have not altered their patterns much and have only expanded their territories. The few species with shorter migrations, and who now summer in their regions' northern fringes, are also shortening their southern migration, remaining in marginal conditions year-round. These species include the Costa's, Anna's, and Allen's hummingbird.

Here's what the migration looks like with some more familiar landmarks.

The male rufous begins his trek from central Mexico in January. By mid-May, he has made it to the northern reaches of British Columbia and into Alaska.

He hits Los Angeles about twenty days into his journey, arriving in early to mid-February. Then, he manages to make it to San Francisco in about twelve days, arriving at the end of February. The next leg, to Portland Oregon, is 640 miles (1,030 kilometers), and he manages that part of the trip by mid to late March. However, he is only halfway there. By now, he is starting to experience longer hours of daylight. Portland to Seattle takes five days (175 miles, 282 km), Seattle to Prince Rupert, British Columbia, another 52 days (1,615 miles, 2,602 km). It is mid-May, and the breeding season is in full swing. Along the route, many rufous birds have stopped off, claiming their summer territories. But a few still soldier on to Juneau, 320 miles (517 km) away. They arrive before the end of May.

Meanwhile, ruby is making its own excursion along the easterly part of the continent. After flying 370 miles (600 km) non-stop across the Gulf of Mexico in late January or early February, he slows to a more leisurely pace, averaging at most 25 miles (40 km) each day.

After his marathon, ruby travels from Houston to Oklahoma City in about 22 days, arriving in the middle to the end of February. His next leg is to Topeka, another 300 miles (481 km), or fifteen days, arriving in the first or second week of March. The jaunt to Fargo, North Dakota, takes him 30 days, arriving in the third or fourth week of April, as he waits for flowers to bloom and sapsuckers to open up sap holes for him. Now, moving to Canada, rubies arrive in Winnipeg and Regina around the middle to end of May. It is a slower trip, waiting for flowers to bloom and feeders to be put out. It is another 225 miles (360 km).

This timeline is an oversimplification, because many hummingbirds stop their journeys early to nest and don't complete the entire route. Still, the magnitude of this herculean effort for such a tiny bird becomes more apparent with this timeline in place.

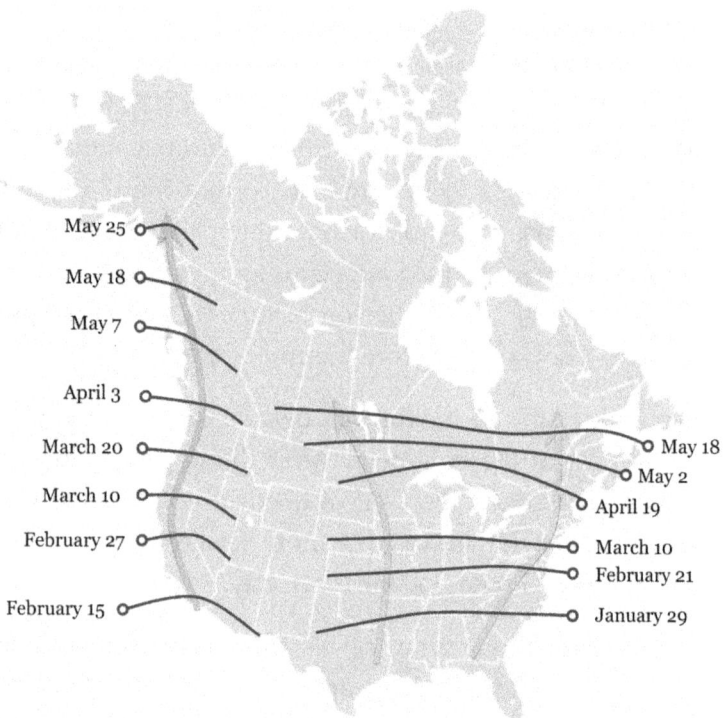

Migration roadmap — approximate dates and migration progress of the rufous hummingbird (Pacific Coast) and ruby-throated hummingbird (East Coast)

But the migration is only a part of the marathon for hummingbirds.

As soon as they arrive, the males must find a territory to defend, and it must be very desirable to the female. It must have a ready supply of food with suitable nesting habitat. Then, each male must fight off a never-ending series of challengers who want his spot. As well, he must spend days dazzling his chosen mate with his prowess.

But for him, the marathon ends after mating. After that, he merely hangs out and eats, continuing to defend his hard-earned food supply.

The female's marathon never ends.

3

MATING SEASON

The three-month spring migration marathon leads into more months of hard work constructing nests and raising chicks, and then another three-month fall migration. There is no downtime for the female until she is wintering in the south. It's no small wonder that she spends her winters apart from the males.

She will complete this annual series of marathons, along with the slightly lazier males, an average of five times. A few may last longer, but not many. While the average lifespan of a hummingbird is three to five years, the oldest ruby in the wild was recorded at nine years, the oldest in captivity 14 years.

Many people believe the hummingbird lifespan in the wild may actually be longer than three to five years, but only a few wild hummingbirds have been found living past the age of ten. Because the immature males and the females look alike, we might incorrectly assume that we are seeing the same birds year after year. However, if we observe them daily and see their individual quirks and habits emerge, we can learn to differentiate specific birds. It is only then we can appreciate how short their lifespan really is.

In deference to the never-ending work of the female, she, like her human counterparts, actually lives slightly longer than the male. It seems that hard work pays off, and the repeated pattern of raising young and migrating huge distances north and south each year does not shorten her lifespan.

Imagine a small, overly-enthusiastic child on a swing set. They push and pull, going higher and higher. Soon, they are level with the chain, building up more and more speed. Finally, at their highest point, they somehow manage a swing that completes almost two-thirds of a circle. Now imagine that same motion, and that same determined enthusiasm, with the male hummingbird replacing the child. This is the mating dance of many hummingbirds.

In early summer, male ruby-throated hummingbirds fly this 'swing' pattern in the air, time and time again, towards a branch on which the female is perched, coming ever closer to her. The pendulum-like swings are an attempt to impress her with his flight prowess, and these swinging arcs may be 50 to 100 feet deep. During this display, the male makes a rapid tik-tik-tik sound with his wings. He makes this same sound during his dives, spreading adding in a faint whining sound by spreading and shutting his outer tail feathers.

The Anna's male even makes sure that he is oriented toward the sun in such a way that his bedazzling iridescent plumage is shown off to the most excellent effect. First, he lures the female into a position that gives her the best view by finding a stage with the optimal seating orientation for his audience of one. Then, to augment the performance, he arcs in such a manner that, as he swoops close, the sunlight hits him perfectly and shines directly at the female.

The Costa's goes a step beyond. Flaring its gorget – the feathers of its neck and throat – in a colorful display similar to the tentacles of a squid. Only his feathers shine an iridescent purple as he dives slowly toward and close to the female. Then he hovers, showing off his fine dress.

It has all the flavor of a thinking being, or an artistic exhibition, rather than an instinctive animal behavior.

Ready to put on a show — male Costa's hummingbird

Sometimes, the female is courted while in flight; other times, she is at rest, perching. There really is no wrong time for the male to intrude on the female to show off. Eventually, she chooses.

Preparing for this display was part of the reason why males rushed ahead to the summer territory to claim the best spot. Of course, there were practical reasons to surge ahead of the competition and the females. The best territory to display also needs to be the best feeding area.

This early part of the summer season is also a time for feasting on new nectar, sugar-water, and insect food sources. Because many hummingbirds 'remember' where those prime feeding areas are, they return year after year, close to the place where they were hatched and raised. As a result, they become familiar with the location and timing of every food source and the times of the season when these are most abundant. They also know how long it takes a given flower to rejuvenate its nectar supply as well as the time of day they can expect the greatest bounty of small insects.

This is a demonstration of the innate ability of animals to recall and map their environment and is not fully understood by researchers. Scientists are reluctant to claim that 'thinking' plays a role here, given that in their first season, with no prior experience, hummingbirds know when, how, and where to migrate. However, the cognitive abilities of birds and their unique brain structures, dense with neural connections, are well known to scientists[1]. With the largest brain in comparison to body size of any bird, it's hard to believe the hummingbird's ability to remember the location and timing of every flower (and feeder) in their territory isn't a sign of their intelligence.

While the edges of forested areas remain the most popular summer 'pick-up' spots, hummingbirds are becoming more and more acclimatized to humans. They are often seen doing their rhythmic swing-dance and taking up residence in suburban settings and backyards.

Backyards have slowly become the best feeding areas for many hummingbirds. They count on sugar-water feeders in the gardens and planted flowers that produce the best nectar, generate the most insects, and offer a significant amount of shelter from the elements and predators. It illustrates how symbiotic relationships can develop between humans and nature to the benefit of both.

Rufous hummingbirds only grudgingly take up residence in human territory, although this happens more often in remote, mountainous areas of Washington, British Columbia, and Alaska. Rubies, though, are found in almost every city east of Montana and British Columbia. They feast on sugar-nectar and ornamental flower gardens while fending off the most dangerous urban predator: the house cat.

When the birds choose to live in our backyards, we become privy to secrets of how they live that we could only guess at before. Their courtship is often on full display, and there is a wonderful range of demonstrations of prowess across many of the hummingbird species. As populations increase, we can peer more closely into their lives.

The mating dances and courtship do not last long; hummingbird mating is as fast as their flights and their dives. It typically lasts only three to five seconds. That's a small fraction of the time spent on finding suitable courtship sites, displaying, diving, and vocalizing, which may last as long as three weeks.

Afterward, the female is left with the task of finding a good neighborhood, building the nest, laying two eggs, brooding them for eleven to eighteen days (depending on species), rearing & feeding the family, then starting once again. On the other hand, like promiscuous humans the male may seek out another female and repeat the process once he has achieved his goal. While it may seem like an irresponsible, carefree lifestyle to humans, he will also have to search out and defend a new feeding territory for every mate, once again taking on all challengers.

There are very few species of hummingbirds that form pair bonds. The exceptions are species such as the violet-ear hummingbird, which bonds for the season but not for life. In this specific case, the male contributes to the brooding and feeding of the young.

As you might expect, hummingbirds do not have powerful calls or voices, yet several species rely on sound as part of the courting ritual. The rufous, for example, produces the loudest sound of any North American hummingbird, even though it is one of the smaller members of the hummingbird family. Being also the most aggressive of the North American species, it seems intuitive that it would also be the loudest. Its sounds, however, are not produced with vocal cords but with its tail feathers[2].

As the rufous reaches the lowest point of its courtship dive, it spreads its tail feathers. The wind, rushing over these feathers, causes them to vibrate, and as they strike each other, they produce a thrumming sound, not unlike an out-of-tune guitar. Depending on the species and tail length, the sound can be described as a whir, whistle, or chirp. Why the female seems attracted to the loudest male is a mystery, even in the human realm.

Anna's hummingbirds and buff-bellied hummingbirds are the exceptions. They actually have songs that are easy on human ears and pleasing to prospective mates. While the speed of these songs can make them challenging to catch at first, the Macaulay Library[3] is a great resource to help you recognize them in your backyard with a little practice.

When female hummingbirds arrive at the summer breeding grounds, they assess the food supply and evaluate potential nesting sites. This is also the time when the ranking and rating of male suitors begins. While the females might appreciate the flight wizardry, calls and songs, tail fluttering, chest fluffing, and deep dives of a showoff, they are also realists. They need to know which males were smart enough to pick, and are tough enough to defend, the best feeding site.

After all, once he departs, she will have to feed her young on her own. She passively watches the exhibition of the males as she starts building her nest. There is not much of a window open to her between breeding and laying eggs – just one day. So, if she agrees to mate, she must already have the nest ready. Then, after laying between one and three eggs, she incubates the eggs and raises the young.

In recent years, ruby-throated hummingbirds have produced two broods in a season with greater frequency. This is happening even in the northern part of their range, where summer is shorter, and is attributed to the abundance of feeders and the changing North American climate. As with any wild animal population, if all the other environmental conditions are right, they will increase in number, so long as they have a regular food supply. It happens with coyotes when rabbits are abundant, wolves when deer or elk are abundant, and even geese when grain fields are abundant. In fact, the current Canada goose population is higher than it was in 1900!

The popularity of backyard feeders and the trend of planting native backyard flora have allowed the hummingbird population in North America to increase in size. It is one of the few modern-day ecological successes where the average person has contributed, and which anyone can easily join in. While other animals are becoming endangered, only a few species of hummingbirds are currently in decline, and only two have gone extinct in the past four decades.

> *In the 1800s, hummingbirds were hunted for their plumage, but now under the Migratory Bird Treaty Act, all migrating birds are protected[4]. As with a few other animals such as the*

beaver, the high society of Europe were so ravenous for the latest styles and accents from the New World that they paid little to no regard to the serious impact their fashion trends were having on hummingbird populations. A dramatic drop in population ensued, with the use of hummingbird feathers in hats, hair styles, and even household accents. Outrage over the cruelty of these popular styles prompted the formation of the first Audubon and conservation societies in the 1890s. The movement was successful, and the use of tropical bird species and their feathers rapidly declined.

There are common mating rituals for most species of hummingbirds, just as there are common rituals for people in the dating scene. And also, like the cultural and regional differences among humans, there are differences between species of hummingbirds. One thing that seems constant in both humans and hummingbirds is that in both species, groups of males like to prance, preen, be loud and showy, and jostle to garner the female's attention. Like female humans, the female hummingbird seems to be a little disdainful of the male until she finally chooses. Here are some notable examples.

Anna's Hummingbird

For this species, the female is wooed by the male's singing rather than his dancing. It is a thin and squeaky song, drawn over about ten seconds. As backup pick-up techniques, the males resort to high dives from above 130 feet. Both sexes mate with several other species.

. . .

Bahama Woodstar

Males use two different techniques to attract the female. 'Shuttle displays' involve periods of side-to-side flights and aerial dives. In between the first and second shuttle segments, the male hovers over the watching female.

The whole time he displays, the male gazes at the female: he has learned that eye contact is essential. Occasionally, the male will snap his tail in the middle segment, then beat his wings rapidly to make a trill sound. Slowly, the male works his way closer to the female.

Aerial dives are less frequent, but zig-zag climbs are typical.

Black-Chinned Hummingbird

This species is known to crossbreed with other species, such as the Anna's, lucifer, broad-tailed, rufous, and Costa's hummingbirds. Oddly, the males and females use different habitats from one another for breeding and living. The males become more and more belligerent as the mating season progresses.

Like some other species, the male uses diving displays and noises from its feather arrangement as it dives to impress the female.

Blue-Throated Mountain Gem

The female of this species is more forward, singing during the breeding season to attract males.

Letting her lead — male blue-throated mountain gem waiting to be impressed by a female

Calliope Hummingbird

The male hovers with an accelerated wingbeat, creating a buzzing sound, with throat feathers flared in front of the female. He climbs to 60 feet, then, calling out, he dives, making a noise with his tail feathers.

Costa's Hummingbird

The male performs a series of swoops and arcing dives, using the sun to show off his plumage to his advantage. Each dive comes within inches of the female while she passively looks on. The plunge will be accented by a high-pitched shriek produced by the tail. Then, the male will perch and vocalize with a similar sound to that produced by his tail.

Lucifer Sheartail

The male hovers high above the female, then dives, with his tail feathers making a snapping sound at the bottom of the dive. He then flies away, creating a different snapping sound with his tail feathers forked. This display lasts 30 to 45 seconds and may be repeated several times.

4

NESTING

Female hummingbirds are the ultimate in single parents. Not only are they burdened with hatching their eggs and raising the young, but they also must build the family home from scratch, all alone. If a female opts to raise two broods, she is generally obliged to create two separate nests.

For every species, the nests are built by the female while the male is courting her. For most, the nests are used only once. By building compact nests, these birds are more able to protect their young from the elements. In addition, they can more easily conceal these small nests from predators or place them in such precarious places that the predators cannot reach them.

The females are so intent on raising a family that they begin building shortly after arriving at their northern migration site. Rufous females begin nest building within three days of arriving. Others build before they look for a mate or, at worst, while entertaining the male's attention. They will breed just as the nest building is finished.

Ruby-throated hummingbirds are expert multi-taskers and may lay eggs in a second nest while still feeding the young in the first one. Since it takes about a week to build a nest, there is a week of the female frantically feeding the young from the first brood while working on her second nest and allowing a male to court her all at the same time.

This almost overwhelming period of activity requires a constant source of food, so she likely only undertakes a second brood when environmental conditions are perfect.

Marvel of engineering – ruby-throated hummingbird sitting in a nest of small leaves held together by spider silk.

Hummingbird nest styles are as varied as the number of species. Each species adds its personal flair and style to nest design, often prompted by available materials, nesting location, and local environmental conditions.

No hummingbird, though, builds its nest in nesting boxes or containers of any sort. The confined space is not conducive to quick getaways. It is an invitation for predators to feast on eggs, young chicks, or even adults. Any attempt to entice a hummingbird to nest in an artificial structure, no matter how pretty, would do the bird a disservice.

It is challenging to find hummingbird nests in their natural habitat, so well do the birds construct and conceal them. Many times, people have confused the funnel webs of varieties of brown spiders with hummingbird nests. Interestingly, the hummingbird does use spider silk, if available, to build its nest. Some of the nests are constructed as high as ninety feet off the ground. They are so tiny that, at that height, they would barely be visible. At their largest, they generally are only one and a half inches in diameter.

These tiny nests are very well camouflaged, built with some of the materials of the tree in which they are built. Often, they are located in thorny bushes or very leafy shrubbery. Most nests are cup-shaped and a little bit stretchy to allow for the growth of the chicks. Each nest is a soft and cozy sanctuary for little humming babies. Some materials in the nests can include feathery grasses, cotton fibers, feathers, spider webs, moss, fuzz from seed pods like cottonwood, and dandelion fluff.

> *Compare the hummingbird nest to an eagle nest. Eagle nests are five to seven feet wide and four feet deep. Year after year, the eagles add more on, and the nests can sometimes reach ten feet in diameter. The nest is a very rough structure, made of branches and sticks. Meanwhile, the hummingbird nest is the size of a thimble, is somewhat elastic, and weighs just a few grams.*

Because they are so small, the nests have to be protected, either by location or design, from winds and rains. At the same time, they must be out of reach of predators such as squirrels, snakes, vermin, and other birds. Unfortunately, as hummingbirds move into urban neighborhoods, cats become their primary predators, climbing trees and shrubs to get at the young.

Urban hummingbirds have become opportunists when building nests. Loose strings from clothes on a line, dryer lint discarded in open garbages, and even fine pet hair is scrounged to build nests. The first round of nest-building for the ruby-throated hummingbird in Canada coincides with the falling of the cottonwoods' soft cotton fluff, making perfect nest material for the rubies. To assist these birds in finding nesting material, you can place your dryer lint on a branch or stump where it can be easily found.

Hummingbirds prefer to build their nests in thick shrubbery or leafy trees, five to ten feet off the ground in the crook of a small branch. However, they have been discovered in flower baskets, security cameras, clotheslines, tennis nets, and lawn décor. Broad-billed hummingbirds construct their nests loosely (for a hummingbird) and often use clotheslines, nets, and decorative lighting wires as anchors.

Ruby nests tend to be lower to the ground than those of other hummingbirds along the west coast of North America. They prefer habitats that consist of deciduous trees and forest edges, stream borders, and backyards. They build on slender, descending branches, five to ten feet off the ground. Trees like oak, birch, poplar, and sometimes pine are their favorites. The ruby's nest sits on top of a branch, rather than in the fork like many other hummingbirds.

It is built of thistle or dandelion down, which become available in late May to mid-June, and is held together with spider silk. How hummingbirds can garner the silk without becoming wrapped in the rest of the web is not well understood. Occasionally, she will use pine resin as an adhesive.

Once constructed, the female stamps on the nest floor to pack and stiffen it, but the walls will remain pliable to allow for the growth of the chicks in this tiny pocket.

Next, the female shapes the lip of the cup by pressing it between her neck and chest. Lastly, she camouflages the nest with bits of lichen and moss from nearby trees. The entire process takes six to ten days to complete.

Ruby-throated hummingbirds have started nesting in downtown areas near Los Angeles, California. This is an extension of the western boundary of this little bird's range and places them in the heart of the human population. Like the robin, the Canada goose, and the peregrine falcon, these little birds have shown that they can live comfortably around humans without risk to their population. This adaptability has been a significant contributor to their population growth since the 1960s.

Rufous nests are quite a marvel as well. Rather than building new structures for every brood, sometimes old nests are reused and refurbished in an established, older community. The nests are compact cups of soft materials like spider webs and plant down, grasses and moss. Like the ruby, the rufous camouflages the nest with lichen and moss.

The female begins by weaving a cup of soft, fluffy plant material and catkins. Then, she layers in moss bound together with spider web strands. Like the ruby, this half-walnut-sized nest is built on a downward-drooping twig, but, unlike the ruby, it sits in the branches' fork. The nests are generally about thirty feet in the air, in deciduous trees like Sitka spruce, Douglas fir, maple, or red cedar.

However, in Washington State, clusters of a dozen to twenty rufous nests have been found in a relatively small area. This arrangement is an enigma, since the rufous is notoriously unsocial.

Allen's hummingbirds prefer to build in the crook of a branch in deciduous trees. Their nests have a near-fairy-like quality, appearing to be able to float away in the wind.

Anna's hummingbird gets an extra early start on raising a family each year. In the southern USA, she starts in January, while she waits until March in the north of her range. Her nest is simple: a basic platform built in the crook of a branch.

NESTING 43

Light as a feather – Allen's hummingbird nest with two eggs

Calliopes, in the southwest USA, build a series of nests, one on top of the other, in coniferous trees. They are the condominiums of the hummingbird world, building communities not unlike the barn swallow, up to four stories high. However, they all 'own' their condos, not allowing other calliopes to intrude too closely.

Once they find a favorable location, Costa's hummingbirds may colonize as many as a half dozen nests in a ten-meter radius. Because of this forced socialization, they tend to be quite tame at their nesting sites. These are the 'town builders' of the hummingbird world.

5

RAISING A FAMILY

It's hard not to draw comparisons between the never-ending work that the female hummingbird does to raise a family and the hard work that a human mother does throughout her life.

She times each stage of raising her family perfectly, every step flowing effortlessly into the next. For instance, in the hottest part of the season, she is incubating the eggs, while at the peak of insect population growth, she is feeding her two chicks.

Humans have made her job easier across the continent, providing and maintaining backyard feeders. Consequently, many of the birds now nest very near human populations to capitalize on flower or vegetable gardens and convenient sources of sugar water. This sometimes allows the female to raise two broods in one year.

Once the female has made her nest, then mated, she will lay one or two or, rarely, three eggs. Three eggs marks the limit of her feeding ability and the ability of the natural environment to provide food. Eggs inside the female take about a day to a day and a half to start forming and are laid one to two days apart. The young hatch at the same time, and the female accomplishes this by not starting the incubation period for the first egg completely until the second egg is laid.

Hummingbird eggs are incubated for 11 to 21 days, depending upon the species and the ambient temperature where the female is nesting. That is quite a range, considering that the entire period from nest building to full-fledged adulthood of young is less than a month and a half. Every hummingbird egg is pure white, about the size of a pea.

The ruby-throats take eleven to sixteen days to incubate. The rufous has three eggs more often than most species, with an incubation period of fifteen to seventeen days. Partly, this is due to the more hostile environment in which they live and the resulting higher mortality rates. Anna's hummingbirds, on the other hand, consistently lay two eggs, but because of their migratory stability, they can have two or three broods per year, with an incubation period of sixteen days.

Strangely coincidentally, the ideal incubation temperature for the hummingbird is between 96 and 98.6°F (36.5°C), the same temperature as the human body. In contrast, the body temperature of an adult hummingbird is 107°F (38°C). The mother hummingbird spends about fifty minutes of every hour on the nest, maintaining that human-like temperature.

The chick, like all birds, has a minuscule hook on its beak that helps it peck its way out of the shell. It may take a full day to accomplish this task. Once it emerges, the female has an increased need for vigilance. This tiny, marble-sized offspring is naked, sightless, and helpless. Most of all, it cannot regulate its body temperature, and the mother cannot leave the baby alone for more than a minute or so. This is why multiple eggs must hatch as close together as possible. If the day is exceptionally cold or exceptionally hot, the new chicks can quickly die of exposure.

At birth, the average hummingbird chick weighs 0.62 grams – roughly half the weight of a dollar bill – but will double its weight in seven days. The chick has fought its way into the world, but is completely at the mercy of the elements and reliant on its mother.

This is one of the reasons for building a nest near a good food source: it will take mere seconds for the parent to find food and bring it back for the young. In its first days, the chick needs more protein than nectar to stimulate its rapid growth; this means insects – and lots of them. Twilight and dawn are the best times to hunt, but being near the right trees and bushes provides a convenient bounty in good seasons. Twilight and dawn also are the coolest times of the day, so the mother must be quick. Flowers and feeders are essential for hummingbirds, but having a habitat that encourages insect populations is necessary too.

A hummingbird may need to eat several hundred insects a day to meet its dietary needs, not including supplying any offspring. But how do they use a mouth specialized for sipping nectar from flowers to catch mosquitoes, flies, and spiders? If you have observed other birds like kingfishers, purple martins, or barn swallows do their aerial dances as they pursue and gobble up their bugs on the wing, or seen the ruthless efficiency with which a dragonfly does the same, then in comparison, the hummingbird will seem like the 100-yard dash champion of aerial pursuit.

While quite a few aphids and small insects are taken in with the nectar of the flowers on which hummingbirds feed, most insects that hummingbirds eat are caught in the air. This technique is called 'hawking' in the avian world. Their thin bills are too fragile to grasp, pierce, or tear apart prey and are totally unsuitable for pecking at seeds or shells. Therefore, the hummingbird must swallow their meals whole, often throwing their heads back with a flourish to speed up the process as they rush to their next target.

Scientists have used high-speed cameras to uncover the mysteries of hummingbird hunting. As a bird closes in on its prey and opens wide, its lower beak flexes downward and widens at the base, increasing in surface area. As the beak bends, it pushes up against the jawbone, building up elastic energy. When the time is right, the beak springs shut in a manner reminiscent of a Venus fly trap, quickly trapping anything inside – a unique ability not found in any other vertebrate species[1].

Hummingbirds are also opportunistic fishermen, exploring the webs of spiders and using their ability to hover and deftly maneuver in tight spaces to pluck newly caught insects off their fishing nets.

In the wild, meadows offer a bounty for the ruby-throated hummingbird. That is why they build nests near the edges of forests instead of deep within shelter. Rufous hummingbirds, often found at elevations as high as 12,000 feet, rely on alpine meadow flowers and abundant, tiny flies and gnats in their environment.

All hummingbird species' new hatchlings are born naked and blind, with short, stubby beaks. This makes feeding the chicks easier for the mother, since the newly hatched young are voracious eaters. They eat every 20 minutes, and the mother is forced to search for food often and quickly in the first few days. In addition, chicks feed primarily on insects instead of sugar-water as they grow, making things even more difficult for the mothers.

While in the nest, the young instinctively know not to soil their beds. They raise their rears and shoot projectiles of liquid waste over the lip of the nest. This is a defensive adaptation, as the odor would be sure to attract predators.

To carry enough food for two without making too many trips, the hummingbird mother can store what she catches or drinks in a pouch in her neck, known as a crop. Every bird has a crop, and mother hummingbirds use it as a shopping bag, reducing the number of trips she must make when her young are most vulnerable. She will regurgitate the nectar, sugar-water, and insects directly into the open mouths of her babies.

It does not take long for those babies to develop pin feathers, then full immature plumage. Most species only remain in the nest for 18 - 24 days. A week or so before fledging, when their feathers become large enough to allow for flight, the young start to test their wings and gain strength. To reduce the risk of accidentally lifting off in a premature departure, they tightly grip the floor or lip of the nest as they practice beating their developing wings.

> *Hummingbird wings articulate. They are attached only at the shoulder, allowing the wing to pivot more readily than other birds. It gives them lift and mobility in every direction. Unlike most birds, which only generate lift on the downward motion of each vertical stroke, hummingbirds are constantly rotating their wings so that each direction of their back and forth horizontal stroke generates lift and propels them. The flexibility of their shoulder joint allows for quick adjustments to direction, in order to provide lift at whatever angle they need, almost instantaneously.*

But the strength the young hummingbirds will need to move their wings at a high enough speed must be developed before they leave the nest. The pectoral muscles that move their wings will make up a quarter of the adult hummingbird's weight. Eventually, the hummingbird will be able to easily outdo the acrobats and aerobatics of the best troupe of Cirque du Soleil aerialists, performing backwards somersaults and changing direction quicker than the eye can see. Hummingbirds can:

- hover like a dragonfly,
- make pinpoint attacks on insects like a falcon,
- fly inverted to reach into dangling flowers,
- fly with their rear (their feet, really) extended like a hornet about to sting, and

- fly in reverse.

Yet their unique articulated wing design does not seem to have many drawbacks, as hummingbirds can still speed along at 25 miles per hour (40 kph). Larger birds with a more conventional wing structure cannot rotate their wing socket to enable hovering.

However, the traditional bird wing does allow most species of fledgling birds to glide safely, however clumsily, for a short distance. On the other hand, if a young hummingbird falters it will likely fall to the ground from its nest, and become prey for predators. Since it cannot use its weak feet to hop or launch itself back into the air, it is an easy target for snakes, lizards, squirrels, or cats.

Once the young chicks are ready to fly, or fledge, they do so. In the first few days and for up to a week, the mother will continue to respond to their mournful cries for food, finding them wherever they have perched or landed and bringing them food. In that time, she attempts to teach them how to find and identify their own food.

As the young grow, they start learning the location of nearby feeders and food sources, and they develop the instinct to return to the same place next year. This pattern may result in even more flowers, more feeders, and more hummingbirds as plants are pollinated, gardens are expanded, and bird populations grow.

For a short time, the mother will allow the young to feed at her chosen feeding spots, but she quickly lets them know they are no longer welcome to live off her bounty, and she will chase them off. She may have another family to raise, and her older children would only usurp the food supply as they matured. But some fledglings are slow learners. It is common to see young hummingbirds attempting to feed off a brightly colored piece of laundry, a colorful shirt on a human, or a painted lawn ornament. But they do eventually learn.

Yet, in the brief interval – a week or so – when the young are still part of a family unit, you can observe very endearing activities. For example, while adult hummingbirds are solitary, fledglings can often be seen huddled together shortly after leaving the nest.

A few days after leaving the nest, the siblings may start to test their power and authority. They will sometimes challenge the mother at the feeder, diving at her to protect 'their' territory. They may engage in mock battles that rarely amount to much. Then, as they tire, they may groom each other and share the same feeder. It is common to see three birds congregated at one feeder, even if another or several are nearby.

But after about a week, the female decides it is time for the young to leave and will drive off the offspring from the area once and for all, chasing them from feeding site to feeding site. Even the male young, not old enough to establish a territory, will yield to the will of their mother.

This is a testing time for the young; if they resist, they will not be able to obtain enough nourishment to survive. So they are left with no choice but to move on, even if it is only for a short distance. Young hummingbirds must continue to eat as much as half of their body weight each day to survive. But they have been provided with the knowledge of how and where to find food. It is up to them to do so on their own.

Yet, like human adolescents and teens, the immature hummingbird will often test the limits of acceptable behavior. After the males depart for the winter, the adult females will almost half-heartedly defend their chosen feeders.

In contrast, the young – male and female – will conduct mock dives and raids around the feeding stations, exasperating the older bird as it guards the site. At this time, late in the season, juveniles will begin coming into their own and attempt to establish their dominance in the hummingbird world. Sometimes they come within inches, until the adult female has finally had enough, attacks, and drives them off for good.

6

RETURNING SOUTH

As the last few weeks of the summer season come to an end, the hummingbirds will drink more often from feeders. The cooler days and nights mean the birds need extra fuel to keep their high-octane bodies energized.

Hummingbirds need more body fat before migrating, but they also need protein to build up their strength. Insects provide that source of protein and will make up as much as fifteen percent of their diets during this time. Our two favorite species pack well for their dangerous southbound trip. Rubies can put on an additional 50% of their weight in fat reserves, and rufous hummingbirds usually put on at least 25%.

Their feeding now starts later in the day because the sun rises later, and ends earlier as darkness also falls earlier. As a result, they cannot afford to stray far from their food source, and the fights that mark the presence of the males in prime territory become less and less intense.

Ruby-throated hummingbird females will defend, aggressively, a backyard feeder late in the season after her young have fledged. It is commonly assumed that only the male hummingbird is territorial, due to a focus on mating territory early in the summer, but the female must also maintain and defend a territory in order to secure a food source so that she can fatten up before the southward migration.

Males do not build up the same quantity of fat reserve as the females do, since they leave earlier, and many blooms and insects are still available along the route. Still, both males and females time their daily travel with the weather and the availability of food. Sometimes they shorten their flights to just a dozen miles or so as they forage for available food, seek shelter from the cold, and avoid contrary winds. Still, they manage to arrive at their winter grounds almost exactly the same day each year.

A few of each year's hummingbirds will begin their first southward migration shortly after reaching young adulthood. Usually, the males leave about ten days ahead of the females, who depart on their own schedule over the span of about two weeks.

A major problem for a southbound hummingbird in the autumn (fall) is that most plants bloom earlier in the season, and pollinated flowers have already converted to seeds. This makes finding food that much more difficult, and insects become vital as well as feeders. While many people claim that hummingbirds are 'following' the available food as they migrate, very often the food has already disappeared even before they arrive.

No hummingbird flocks with others, since there is no practical advantage to doing so. Each sets out on its journey, with its own timetable, following a route already ingrained in it instinctively, and none is the same as any other hummingbird's. Most males have already departed by late August, as the end-of-season feeding frenzy has prepared the hummingbirds for the long, southbound flight.

Unlike larger birds like geese, crows, or gulls, hummingbirds do not engage in 'test flights' to familiarize themselves with migration protocol. As a result, their learning curve is short, and since they fly alone they must rely on their own reserves, strength, stamina, and instinctive survival skills.

Until they develop those survival skills, young hummingbirds are more at risk of being taken by a predator than adults, who become much warier. You can see the nervousness in the late-season birds, cautiously approaching and feeding at the feeders. This time of year, after fledging and before migration, has a steep learning curve for this year's birds. There are false starts and mistakes along the way, and what seems like nervousness, as their behavior can be a little erratic and not to its usual form.

It looks, to us, like the same nervousness we humans feel as we anticipate our winter vacations. We're ready to go, but uncertain if we have everything. Perhaps the young birds are unsure if they have packed on enough fat reserves. Perhaps, like us, they can be apprehensive about the upcoming trip, wary of the unknown to come. There are far more hummingbirds that migrate south than north each year – clear evidence of the higher risk of mortality over the southern winter, where predators are more abundant and active.

Or perhaps we simply are projecting our own emotions onto them, after spending months living side-by-side and developing a connection to their miniature world.

> Scientists suggest that the northern migration of hummingbirds is, in part, dictated by the supply of food emerging along the route. Yet, the food supply is waning as they fly south, and the birds have difficulty keeping up with the retreating edge of the flower supply, while the insect population is also decreasing.
>
> The male hummingbird leaves two weeks ahead of the female on the northern migration to stake out prime courting, breeding, and feeding territories. Then, the males also leave for the south two weeks ahead of the females in late summer. But in mid to late August, the majority of winds are blowing up from the south directly into the faces of the early migrating males, making their journey more difficult.
>
> It may be that the females are delayed with a late brood, but even after chicks have fledged, females linger a while longer in the north. Given that the male is not an active parent or partner, could they simply be acting selfishly, rushing to capitalize on the abundant food to the south before it disappears for the winter? Or are they a spearhead or decoy of some purpose, while the females delay and take advantage of a greater preponderance of northwest tailwinds to assist their flight?

It is a lonely return journey without the excitement or urgency of the upcoming breeding season at the southern destination. Nights become longer and colder, even as the birds reach further south into the USA and northern Mexico. After becoming accustomed to fourteen hours of sunlight or more in Canada, they now see less than twelve hours of daylight for the bulk of their journey. With longer, cooler nights, they are burning even more energy while resting and waiting for dawn.

Torpor is a survival mechanism that allows hummingbirds to endure cooler nights in the spring and fall. Even in ideal climates and during warm summers, the hummingbird's hyper-charged metabolism could burn through all of its energy reserves overnight. So in the evening, the bird's metabolism slows dramatically. The heart, typically pumping at 1,000 beats per minute, slows to around human levels of 50 beats per minute. The lungs, relying on 150 breaths per minute during the day, almost entirely stop. Their body temperature, normally over 100 degrees, drops by up to 50 degrees, matching ambient conditions. Hummingbirds in torpor can appear dead.

This process is incredibly effective at conserving energy, reducing their metabolic rate by up to a factor of 50, and allowing some species to survive in higher elevations of the mountains or the cool coastal air in Alaska. Torpor is similar to a frog entering and leaving hibernation with each thaw and freeze of spring, but unlike the process taking place in the frog, torpor does not involve chemical changes. It depends entirely on the temperature.

The hummingbird does not emerge immediately and quickly from torpor. As they wake, they begin rapidly vibrating and flapping their wings, warming their body the same way you might pull-start a small engine. It may take as much as half an hour for a hummingbird to recover and begin feeding, or to resume flying south again in the morning.

Hummingbirds are not alone in their journey: there are millions of birds migrating higher above them. These birds, too, must feed, and occasionally a swift predator will take a hummingbird. Mostly, though, the weather and the availability of food will determine if the hummingbirds survive the trip. Given the magnitude of the flights for our two protagonist species, rufous and ruby, they need every resource they can access to continue to thrive and survive. However, most migrating hummingbird species have an advantage in fall migration over their spring journey: wind.

Winds coming out of the north or northwest begin to blow more frequently as the late summer progresses. In September, northerly winds can be quite ferocious. This is a great assist to a small bird, even though the hummingbirds rarely fly above the treetops. Just the same, cold weather generally blows in from the north, so hummingbirds can more readily surf the winds ahead of a cold front.

Rufous hummingbirds are already well adapted to colder weather, and they can endure lower temperatures than any other hummingbird. This adaptation has resulted in more extended north and south journeys each year; however, rufous does get a wind assist in both spring and fall. As the birds return south and reach the western United States, they can loop further to the east and gain the benefit of riding the Great Basin High, a weather system with winds that blow southward in the autumn (fall). But they also risk the early onslaught of cold weather rushing down the valleys between mountain ranges. Being so tiny, even for a hummingbird, this is a risky journey, but one that must be made.

The ruby can anticipate, at best, a tailwind from the north or, at worst, hurricanes that suck rain and wind up from the south or the east. If a hurricane travels through the Gulf of Mexico, the southeast states will experience north-blowing winds on the eastern side of the system, hindering the progress of the ruby. But if the hurricane is further out to sea and skirts the Outer Banks of Georgia, the landward side of the system blows to the south, assisting the ruby. If rubies are caught in the August and September hurricane season, they would be fortunate to be on the west side, sucked down by the counterclockwise rotation of the storm. Those rubies returning from the west and Midwest states and provinces are in that fortunate group. However, if they are returning from the east coast, they will be faced with southerly headwinds and rain.

If a storm blows a hummingbird off course in the spring, it has a long season in which to recover. However, in the fall, an autumn storm may mean death for the delicate bird. Few can survive one night of below-zero temperatures, let alone several.

Unlike the northward migration, when the boldest ruby males attempt to cross directly over the Gulf of Mexico, the birds are in less of a frenzied rush once they reach the southern states. The males have a shorter distance to go than the females, and few of the rubies opt to repeat the risky non-stop flight over the Gulf, instead either wintering in southern Florida or circling the west edge of the Gulf into the Yucatán. Unlike humans, they tend not to be in a rush to reach warmer climates, and instead are only in a panic when heading north in the spring towards the cold.

After nearly three months of flying south, rufous and ruby are back in their winter homes. The remaining eighteen or so migrating species have also completed their journeys for the year. The females left later, and have almost universally taken longer and traveled farther, not bothering to socialize with the males. They will get a well-needed rest, recover, and begin the cycle once again next year.

I hope you enjoyed following the year-long journey with the Rufous and Ruby-Throated hummingbirds.

But the real joy in experiencing the natural world is sharing it with those around us. So before we get into the details of creating a space for hummingbirds around your home, please take a minute and think of anyone else in your life who would enjoy reading this book, and remember to share it with them afterwards.

And if you can't think of anyone right now, the next best thing you can do is leave a review wherever you purchased this book, to help other readers discover it for themselves.

PART II: FEEDERS

Feeding hummingbirds is a symbiotic relationship that goes far beyond the enjoyment we receive. The presence of abundant feeders stimulates greater populations of hummingbirds to move into an area, which helps control insect populations and assists in pollinating even more flowers and plants.

As we observe these little marvels, we are inspired to spend more time outdoors, plant and tend more gardens (including vegetable gardens), and improve our environment. At the same time, it almost appears that the more curious of the hummingbirds are also entertained by us. We find them hovering about our heads, peering as they arc around us, and, in some instances, seemingly demanding that we attend to their feeding needs.

Yet, feeders are simple to maintain and cost very little to replenish. In exchange, the birds are provided with a stable, consistent food source. They also are a constant source of entertainment and information, raising questions and piquing curiosity more than providing answers.

The influence of hummingbirds extends beyond human observers. Biologists believe that the evolution of over a dozen flowering plants along the ruby's territory, over many centuries, occurred almost in lockstep with the growth of hummingbird populations. The shape of both the flowers and the ruby's bills slowly became longer and more tubular as the partnerships flourished.

> *Even though hummingbirds have long tongues, sometimes twice the length of their bills, they don't use their tongues to suck up nectar through their bills like a straw.*
>
> *Their forked tongues are actually fringed with tiny hairs. As a hummingbird extends its tongue, the w-shaped forks expand to gather fluid. Then, as the tongue retracts, it is compressed by the bill. This creates capillary action that naturally pushes fluid upward and into their throats.*

Feeders are often vigilantly guarded by dominant hummingbirds, who mercilessly swoop in and chase away interlopers. This basic territorial response can be interesting to watch, but there may be more behind the scenes if you pay attention.

Often, less dominant or juvenile birds will appear to work together to create an opportunity, in the same way that wolf packs or even orca whales trade off duties so that each can feed. While the dominant hummingbird is busy chasing off a competitor, a third bird perched nearby waits until the guard has flown off a decent distance in pursuit. Only then will it fly down and feed for a few moments. This decoy role may be alternated with other birds and this tactic will become more evident as you learn the behaviors of the birds near your home.

Bird personalities can also begin to emerge at the feeders.

One hummingbird might always take a cautious moment to look around and see if others are waiting to attack, then will insert its beak into one of the holes and draw up the syrup in one sitting, continuing without pause until a bubble of air erupts from the cavity to the top of the feeder jar. That is a lot of liquid for a small bird!

Another might have a more nervous disposition and refuse to perch, constantly fluttering as it feeds.

A third might throw its head back as it swallows, like a person taking their pills in the morning.

Or maybe one is indecisive and always has to try every receptacle in the feeder, at every feeding.

One of the friendlier hummingbirds continues to chirp, squeak, and chatter, even while drawing food up from the feeder. It never stops talking.

And a more health-conscious hummingbird routinely draws a few sips from the sugary feeder, moves to a nutritious flower, and continues back and forth, balancing its taste selection like we humans do between nourishing meals and tasty desserts.

These behaviors all likely have an evolutionary explanation, but the personification of these little marvels is difficult to resist. It is what makes the maintenance of feeders in the summer worthwhile.

7

CHOOSING YOUR FEEDER

Pretty is not the priority for hummingbird feeders, neither is expensive. Aesthetics and status should take a back seat to functionality when selecting hummingbird feeders. Instead, these three primary considerations should guide your purchase: the feeders should be easy to hang, easy to fill, and easy to clean.

Feeders that are well balanced and not overly large are the easiest to hang. However, if they are flared too wide, feeders will swing in the wind. Large feeders may also be awkward to place in an area where other extrusions can brush against or crowd the feeder. Or they may be too heavy to hang on tree branches.

Ease of filling is important for a few reasons. First, the sugary solution is quite sticky. This is not just an inconvenience for us, as any sugar solution on the outside of the feeder will attract insects. Second, a well-designed feeder should have a removable top for filling, even if the bottom also is removable, and a wide opening. Finally, a well-balanced feeder with a flat bottom can be filled by setting it on a counter, rather than holding it up or trying to fill it while hanging. Avoid feeders that cannot stand upright when being filled.

Of the three primary considerations when obtaining a feeder, choosing one that is easy to clean is the most important. Your feeders must be kept clean at all times. If you fail to clean your feeder regularly or do not properly clean it, fungus and molds can quickly develop. These are incredibly harmful to the delicate bodies of hummingbirds. Although they often can detect spoiled food and will avoid the feeder, young hummingbirds and birds whose natural food supply is interrupted may still feed on spoiled sugar nectar.

Exposure to mold can cause the hummingbird's tongue to swell, making it impossible for the bird to feed, and it may slowly and painfully die of starvation. That same infection can be passed on to the chicks by an infected mother, killing them. A feeder should not be designed with hard-to-reach parts, as this makes them difficult to clean. Edges, shallow remote areas, and awkward protrusions can harbor bacteria and mold. The best feeders have a simple throat and body system that can be cleaned easily with a bottle brush. However, cleaning of the exterior is also essential, and feeders that have unnecessary adornments, ridges, and protrusions can be hard to clean, while accumulating dirt and mold.

Along with these design considerations, look for durable feeders. The feeders hang outdoors for five or more months of the year, exposed to the elements. Cheap plastic feeders will fade, making them less attractive to hummingbirds. The plastic may also harden and break down, so the lifespan of the ten-dollar feeder may be a quarter of the twenty-dollar feeder. Plastic surfaces also allow for more mold growth than glass. Many of the cheaper designs have feeding ports that tend to leak and break loose over time. As soon as one port fails, the vacuum seal that holds the nectar in place can leak. This will result in a sticky mess of sugar-water, attracting pests.

Choosing a feeder with five or more feeding stations is generally not a good investment, since the territorial hummingbirds will drive away other birds. However, one hummingbird may flit from one station to the next at each feeding, anticipating that each station is a different flower. Feeders with three or four stations are the most practical.

Hummingbird feeders, unfortunately, are attractive to other birds. Most designs also have perches for the hummingbirds to rest while they feed. Those perches are inviting to birds like finches and orioles, who are attracted to the bright colors and will scare off hummingbirds. These larger birds will often peck at the flower ports, trying to widen them, and can easily damage cheaper feeders. Because these intruding birds are heavier, the feeder may tilt as the large songbirds perch, breaking the air vacuum that holds the syrup inside, and allowing it to leak.

If you put out feeders with perches, consider them sacrificial, and expect that larger birds will use them. At the same time, put out a few perchless feeders in strategic locations, so that only hummingbirds that are hovering can feed at them.

Along with other birds, insects (both flying and crawling) will begin to arrive. While many designs have insect guards or bee shields to deter these pests, there are a few things to consider.

First, ants have an uncanny ability to find and capitalize on feeders. Fortunately, the better feeders have designs that deter and frustrate ants. The thin cord that feeders hang from is barely a speed bump for them. Ant moats, which fit over the cord and are part of many styles of feeders, are relatively effective, but only if the water in them has not evaporated. In uncovered locations, pine needles and bits of debris often fall into the moats, providing the ants with a convenient raft. If your feeder is in a brushy location, the occasional branch may allow ants to gain access. Just the same, ant moats do significantly reduce ant mobility and access to the feeders.

In the late season, bees, wasps, hornets, and even flies will congregate around the feeder. Wasps, hornets, and flies are only after sugar, so regular cleaning will prevent them from visiting that often. Bees, on the other hand, are often looking for water. Aside from drinking, bees use water to dilute honey, cool down their hive, and to feed their larvae. Setting up a nearby bee bath is a simple project that gives bees an alternative to your feeder. Just place a few flat river stones in a shallow dish, with just enough water so that the stones are not fully submerged.

I would strongly recommend against using any chemical pesticides. However, if you choose to use these products, ensure that none of the product reaches the feeder or any locations where hummingbirds might perch or gather nesting materials. Pesticides, insecticides, and insect repellents may be considered 'safe' for use around humans, but even small amounts of these chemicals can seriously harm hummingbirds, damaging their metabolism, nervous systems, and disrupting egg-laying hormones. Eradicating insect populations also removes one of the hummingbirds' key food sources.

Partners in Flight – a conservation group that tracks several species of birds, including hummingbirds – estimates that the rufous population is currently 62% smaller than it was in 1966. Pesticide use along their summer territories has been largely blamed for this decline. Rufouses are adapting, however, and becoming more willing to use urban feeders and gardens.

Generally, each feature that benefits the hummingbird comes with a negative trade off. For instance, perches generally have more advantages than disadvantages, as they give hummingbirds a place to rest, but they also make your feeder more convenient for other (non-hovering) bird species.

Tradeoffs such as these may result in you needing to replace a feeder or two each year or trying out a few different options until you find the design that works best for you.

If you are putting out multiple feeders in different locations, use a variety of designs. At the beginning and end of the season, when there are fewer birds, put out smaller sized units, since they will need to be cleaned frequently.

In the peak of the summer, a larger sized feeder may still need to be refilled every other day. Once the chicks arrive, demand increases substantially. The larger feeders are effective in higher bird traffic areas, so watch where the birds prefer to feed and place the biggest feeders there. Planning the size and type of feeder is a bit of a balancing act that is being altered constantly throughout the season.

While there is no perfect number of feeders to put out, if this is your first year attracting hummingbirds, you should start with just one. It might take hummingbirds a few weeks to find it, and you still need to replace the sugar-water mixture regularly, whether it's been emptied or not. Depending on the species you attract, you might be able to place several feeders close together, or may have to spread them apart to avoid too many fights.

Lastly, there are two primary types of feeder – vacuum and saucer – as well as three less common styles and purely decorative options. Any style can have ant moats or insect guards built into the design or added to the structure.

Most feeders are vacuum style, also called inverted-bottle feeders. In this design, the liquid in the feeder is prevented from leaking out by the air pressure above it. These feeders consist of a glass or plastic jar or bottle and a base with flower-shaped feeding ports. The advantage of this type of feeder is that it is generally easier to clean. Hummingbirds can also easily get to the sugar-water, as the nectar is very close to the port openings. The downside is that if the feeding ports leak, that means the vacuum seal is broken, and most likely, the feeder has to be replaced. Bees and other insects also have an easier time getting to the sugar solution, unless the feeder is designed with bee-guards. Some designs require you to fill the bottle upside-down, attach the base, and then flip the feeder over, which can occasionally get messy.

Vacuum feeder — with male hummingbird using the perch and saying hello to the photographer

The saucer style feeder has all of the liquid contained in a flattened bowl. The feeder ports are on top, allowing the hummingbirds easy access to the syrup. These are less stable than the vertical vacuum feeders; however, they come apart easily for simple cleaning. These often hang by a center stalk or reinforced rope/cable. The advantage of this design is that it does not rely on a vacuum seal. There is also some separation between the ports and the nectar to prevent insects from accessing the nectar. The disadvantage is that hummingbirds generally prefer the more convenient vacuum style that is easier to drink from.

Saucer feeder — with male hummingbird using the perch and ignoring the photographer

While it would seem that vacuum feeders have the advantage, saucer-style feeders do have their place. So if you are trying to keep away bees, larger birds, or don't have the budget for a more durable vacuum-style feeder, the saucer style might be the way to go.

The less common feeder styles are venturi (throttle neck), window feeders, test tube feeders, and decorative feeders. Other options like wearable feeder rings or glasses might be fun occasionally but are not reliable enough to be used on their own.

Venturi feeders have an hourglass shape that serves more of an aesthetic purpose than a practical one. As a result, they are among the most popular mid- to low-priced feeders.

Window feeders are very popular in urban settings. Their primary purpose is to allow humans to view, up close, the feeding antics of hummingbirds. The window feeders are often smaller and made of lighter plastic, and affix to glass using suction cups. Some, however, have cords and hooks that can screw directly into the window frame. They are generally not very durable and are less expensive than saucer feeders, but they can be useful in tight spaces or to prevent serious window collisions (see the upcoming section on Window Collision Mitigation).

Test tube feeders are small, thin, test-tube-shaped feeders with a brightly colored tip to attract the hummers. They are also great for small spaces. They can be hidden among the taller plants in your garden, on patios, or as supplemental feeders along pathways. They are so small that they require refilling often, but allow you to see the birds up close if placed near a seating area or window. They rarely have perches or ant moats.

Decorative feeders often are made of hand-blown glass or similar material. These can look spectacular and provide great accents to an outdoor space. Still, they often don't disassemble easily, and it may be difficult to scrub the inside properly. They usually don't last more than one season and are primarily intended for aesthetic purposes for humans, and should not be used regularly. Being challenging to clean makes them prone to mold and bacteria, as well as putrid sugar water on hot days.

8

PLACING YOUR FEEDER

The location of your feeders will determine, in a very significant way, the popularity of those feeders with your hummingbird residents. This is because the birds require safe, consistent, quality food and a convenient 'table' to eat at. Hummingbird feeders are the bird equivalent of a fast-food restaurant. As with humans, the closest option that meets those requirements will end up being the most popular.

However, choosing the perfect location doesn't have to be complicated. Placing your hummingbird feeders requires only a few basic rules.

First, feeders should not be placed in direct sunlight, as the bright, hot sun hastens the deterioration of the nectar within. Unsheltered areas also expose the bird to excessive heat and cold. Liquid in direct sun may heat to over 120°F (50°C) because of absorption of the sun's rays on the red material. There is also no need to completely shelter feeders from rain, as hummingbirds don't mind a light shower now and then.

Feeders should not be placed in closed-in areas. Birds will not feed in tight spots because of the heightened risk of attack from predators and other territorial hummingbirds. Do not place feeders in thick foliage or too close to the ground either: hummingbirds only feel comfortable if there are multiple escape routes.

Hummingbirds are used to feeding off both low and higher-growing plants, but the ideal height range is between five and ten feet. So long as the feeder is easily visible, placing them strategically throughout the garden or even on the edges of your deck will be effective. Hanging feeders from poles or solid structures is recommended, as they can be too heavy for small branches on the outer regions of trees when filled. If you hang a small shade canopy over a feeder in a sunny location, it will act as an umbrella in the rain, as well.

Lastly, feeders must be properly spaced from glass or reflective surfaces. They must either be placed close by, within three to five feet, or else at least thirty feet away. This spacing will reduce collisions (more on that later).

Placing feeders where you can easily observe them satisfies your desire to be entertained by these tiny marvels, but that should be the least of your considerations. While there are feeders that attach directly to a window, the presence of people on the other side of the glass can spook the birds.

One of the common questions about placing hummingbird feeders is whether other songbird feeders should be placed nearby. There is both a short and a long answer to that question.

Placing other bird (like songbird) feeders nearby can attract the attention of predators, since those birds will often also nest nearby. While hummingbirds can recognize whether another bird is a predator or not, sometimes larger birds will attempt to use (and damage) the hummingbird feeders. So, the short answer is, songbird feeders should not be placed nearby, and moved to open lawn spaces or away from the garden.

The long answer is that the songbirds can act as buffers for the hummingbirds in some situations, since they are slower and more obvious targets. That means that a predator like a cat might go for the bigger birds, and will happen upon hummingbirds less often. However, overhead predators like kestrels, falcons, and hawks may take up permanent outposts nearby, posing a greater risk to young hummingbirds and nests.

There is evidence that hummingbirds can become comfortable with some types of aerial predators, nesting in the territory of larger predatory birds that ignore the bite-sized hummingbirds. But a well-balanced nature garden should invite a variety of small and large birds. The placement of songbird feeders in the vicinity offers both advantages and threats. Diversity is great for the ecosystem, but there is always a price to pay for this diversity.

9

WINDOW COLLISIONS

You can do many things to reduce the frequency and severity of bird collisions with windows – not just hummingbirds, but all birds. As we become more urbanized, we turn to large buildings with abundant glass and reflective surfaces. When communities are built on bird flyways and migratory routes, we increase the likelihood of bird strikes and deaths. Hummingbirds can easily break their delicate beaks if they hit a window, and their chances of survival after such an injury are abysmal.

If we are going to intrude on nature, we have a duty to intrude in a way that does a minimum of harm. This can be accomplished on a large scale by compelling builders to take mitigation steps in their design and architecture, and on a small scale by assuming individual responsibility. Birds strike windows for four reasons:

1) they see through the glass to the other side of the building, and interpret that there is no impediment to flying directly to the forest or an open route on the other side;

2) the reflection of foliage or open sky from behind the bird creates an illusion that the surrounding greenery from the environment around them is continuing in the glass;

3) the birds see attractive items inside the room and attempt to approach them; or

4) they see their reflection as a threat or challenge from another male and attack the reflective surface.

Clearly, there are many options and solutions to reduce bird strikes. If you want to develop an inviting and safe habitat for birds and, specifically, hummingbirds, consider how you can adopt and adapt these suggestions to suit your situation.

Anywhere you are planning to place a feeder, make sure to look through the nearby sets of windows and see if there is a clear visual path through the building. If there is, options to remove this path include:

- Closing the blinds or draperies on either side of the building.
- Placing decals strategically on the glass.
- Installing insect screens or horizontal stripes.

Wind chimes, whirligigs, and other ornaments can also help break up the illusion and reduce bird impacts. Backlighting can enhance the perception that a clear path is available for the birds, so keep interior lights off, particularly at dusk.

When the sun is at a specific angle, reflections will appear real to birds. Before choosing a location for feeders, check your windows at the key times of day (dawn and dusk) for

WINDOW COLLISIONS

reflections of vegetation or sky. Make sure that your outdoor lights do not create a mirror effect on glass or reflective metallic surfaces. Decals, screens, and striping can again be used to destroy this illusion. Decals of predators are particularly effective. Put life-sized colored (not dark) decals of a bird of prey on the window, or use a figurine near the window to scare away hummingbirds.

On some beaches, you will see wooden eagles perched on poles to scare away seagulls or hawks at the edge of a garden with sunflowers in it to deter blackbirds and grackles. You might try such an approach, but be sure to move the decal or figurine occasionally so that the hummingbirds do not become accustomed to it. Alternatively, awnings or shutters can be used to block the reflections.

To avoid having hummingbirds seeking out items inside your home that are visible through the large windows, you can make the following adjustments. Move your indoor plants to corners or areas of a room that do not appear to have open space. Do not use floral wallpaper, drapes, or other decorations on walls near or opposite large windows. Turn off unnecessary lights (or set them on timers) as unnatural light can cause problems for birds, who can also see ultraviolet light. Grow lights used for indoor plant arrangements can draw the birds to those plants.

Aggressive hummingbirds can appear throughout the summer season, but most attacks on each other occur at breeding time. Hummingbirds cannot recognize their reflection, and they may immediately try to attack. To reduce the danger, either place bird feeders close enough to windows (within 3 feet), or further away (more than 30 feet away), so any unavoidable collisions won't be at high speed.

As a final, more expensive and permanent solution, you could install UV-reflective glass, etched or sandblasted glass, or fritted glass to break up the visual line of sight for the birds.

In the unlikely scenario that a hummingbird makes it inside of your home and is unable to escape, don't panic, and just follow this simple procedure.

First, identify the state that the hummingbird is in. Initially, if a bird believes that it is trapped, it may instinctively seek out a high perch to keep out of reach from predators and easily identify any other threats. Or, it may panic and desperately seek an exit, often running into windows, screens, or see-through curtains. This may injure the hummingbird, and often the fragile bills are at risk.

Finally, after a long period of high stress and no food, the trapped hummingbird will become exhausted. Hummingbirds can't walk or hop. Their feet are too delicate and dainty. If they need to, they can lift off and turn on a perch, seeming to shuffle, but their legs have long ago evolved as almost unnecessary appendages, with the exception of clinging to a nest when they are young, and anchoring them to a perch. A hummingbird too stunned, exhausted, injured, or otherwise unable to fly is essentially immobilized.

WINDOW COLLISIONS

Next, remove any perceived threats to the hummingbird. This includes excited children, pets, and any sources of movement or lights.

Then, create clear paths to the exit. Cut off any alternate routes that might trap the bird or give them hiding places like doors or cupboards, remove any distractions like red colored objects, and turn off indoor lighting to make the exit as bright as possible. Often having an exterior porch light or flashlight turned on at the exit while interior lights are off does the trick. You can also place red objects or a feeder at the exit to lure the hummingbird.

You should not directly touch the hummingbird unless absolutely necessary; instead, use a broom, or another long and soft object, to gently direct them. However, if the bird is stunned and unable to fly, you can gently gather it in your hands and bring it to a feeder. A stunned bird can appear dead or injured for several minutes before recovering, so stay close by and ward off any predators while it is helpless.

However tempted you might be, it is illegal to keep a hummingbird captive as a pet. If you cannot safely remove a trapped hummingbird from your home, contact a local animal control authority.

Common spots where hummingbirds might get trapped inside include garages, sheds, screened-in porches, and playhouses. If hummingbirds end up in your home or in these spots, do a quick check and consider removing any bright red items (like tools, bottles, or flower pots) which might be attracting curious hummingbirds.

10

PREPARING THE NECTAR

Despite our earlier comparison of feeder nectar to fast-food, consider yourself a five-star chef when preparing a homemade mixture for your birds. Take all the care in preparation that you would expect in a fine-dining kitchen when cleaning, handling, storing, preparing, and presenting the hummingbirds' meals.

Firstly, and almost counterintuitively to our five-star attitude, you should only use granulated white sugar in the nectar mix. Store-bought mixes may contain preservatives and dyes, both of which are harmful to the hummingbirds. Honey and artificial sweeteners can also be fatal to hummingbirds. Honey is very susceptible to mold, botulism, and toxins associated with fungi. Similarly, other processed sugars (including confectioner's sugar) are not suitable for the hummingbird.

Remember, the nectar solution you are creating is only intended to supply calories to the hummingbird, not essential nutrients. Hummingbirds will continue to feed at flowers and catch insects even when plentiful feeders are available. We can trust hummingbirds to recognize the need to balance out their diets and meet their nutritional needs.

Although you may be tempted to use 'healthier' substitutes, like organic or raw sugar, this is not actually an improvement.

Organic and raw products are more susceptible to fungus and mold in the same way that honey fosters pathogens. And while these products have been made healthier for humans by concentrating additional vitamins and minerals, this can result in the buildup of excess dietary iron in the hummingbirds' intestines and livers.

Since they are drinking between four and five times their body weight every twelve hours, any changes to the expected concentration of nectar ingredients can be extremely damaging to their digestive system. Other, similar sugar products, like turbinado sugar or brown sugar, are also not acceptable substitutes.

To prepare the mix, use a clean, steel mixing bowl to avoid bacteria. Then, boil the water for a few minutes to kill any pathogens and aid in dissolving the sugar into the solution.

Measure out one cup of granulated white sugar and add it to four cups of water.

The recipe doesn't have to be exact, but do not attempt to adjust this ratio. The 4:1 mixture is designed to mimic the natural sugar content of plant nectar. It is the perfect level of sweetness and caloric density to fuel hummingbirds. Many people believe they are doing the hummingbirds a favor if they mix a 3:1 or even 2:1 water-to-sugar mix, but too much sugar will harm the hummingbird's liver, while too little will not provide the energy that hummingbirds need.

Allow the liquid to cool before filling a thoroughly cleaned feeder. Keep any excess syrup covered and refrigerated to prevent bacteria buildup.

11

CLEANING & MAINTENANCE

The hummingbird feeder requires the most attention and care of all the bird feeders you may have in your backyard. Simply by containing a sugar and water mix, it becomes a magnet for fermentation, mold growth, and insects in the heat of the summer. Each time you refill the feeder, you are likely to find dead insects at the dispensers or even in the water. These decaying insects, along with existing bacteria and the heat of the sun, can ferment or contaminate the feeder liquid.

There are various suggested methods as to how to best clean your feeder, but, like many sources of information available today, some are dangerously wrong. The simplest way to consider the proper cleaning of your bird feeders is to apply that same high-end restaurant standard to your cleaning regimen: heat, soap, scrub, and rinse.

Ignore suggestions that feeders should be sterilized with bleach. That idea is partly based on the desire to clean the film from the glass or plastic and kill mold. After all, bleach works wonders on areas of your home that may have mold and always manages to get surfaces sparkling clean. But we don't eat off those areas. Even the most minuscule amount of bleach can kill a hummingbird, and a perfectly sterile level of cleanliness can be achieved without that level of risk to hummingbirds, or potential harm to yourself.

Vinegar is perfect for cleaning scum off the glass, and rinsing with hot water will remove any vinegar residue. However, vinegar is not a complete answer to the cleaning problem. If you opt to use a vinegar solution as part of the cleaning regimen, let the feeder stand for a couple of hours with the vinegar in it. Then thoroughly scrub with a bottle brush and follow with your regular washing process.

Using soap and warm water carries risks, as well. The soap residue can be very harmful to the birds' stomachs. To some degree, the hummingbirds seem able to detect the soap. They will often shy away from those feeders that have not been thoroughly rinsed, but juveniles may not be so discriminating.

The most effective way to clean the feeder is to use a detergent and very hot water, scrubbing every portion of the bottle, inside and out, with a bottle brush. It is vital to clean the flower feeder ports, as this is where a lot of the mold problems begin. Bathe the feeder in a very hot water bath for twenty minutes, then drain and rinse the feeder bottle again in cool water. Let the bottle air dry (or even dry it in the dishwasher) before refilling.

You may note that this system operates in much the same way as an institutional dishwasher, applying a soapy bath of very hot water and a couple of rinses before air drying

CLEANING & MAINTENANCE

the dishes. Your hummingbirds deserve no less care than the standard that is established by the local health departments for the handling of human food.

Every time you refill your feeders, wash them with hot tap water (not distilled). Most tap water systems are chlorinated to reduce bacteria build-up in the water supply; however, the level of chlorine used is considered safe.

If the outside temperature is over 80°F (26°C), empty the feeders, clean and refill them every three or four days, regardless of whether or not hungry hummingbirds have emptied them. Clean them every two days when the daytime temperature exceeds 90°F (32°C) to prevent spoilage and mold.

While this level of cleaning may seem excessive, more dangerous toxins, such as botulism, become a risk at these temperatures. Suppose the feeders were contaminated from the outside environment, for instance, by songbirds exposed to botulism from other sources. In that case, higher temperatures would promote the growth of fungi and increase the rate of toxin build-up. Another risk of waiting too long between cleanings is the fermentation of the sugar mixture. As curious as you might be, for both the hummingbird's safety and yours, you should do your best to avoid having a drunk rufous buzzing around your yard.

For anyone intimidated by the amount of cleaning and feeding involved here, I can assure you that you are not alone. At first, attracting hummingbirds seemed like a quick and easy way to enjoy some wildlife and freshen up your outdoor space. Now you are slaving away in a kitchen! There is an upside here, though.

Hummingbirds have the ability to recognize and differentiate various humans, shying away from strangers but being particularly cocky around familiar people. They will begin to recognize the person who regularly fills the feeders and will hover around them without fear. While their ability to recognize people is not as well developed as that ability is in crows, ravens, or parakeets, it won't take long before they start giving their compliments to the chef and allow you a closer view.

12

COMMON PROBLEMS & SOLUTIONS

WHY IS MY FEEDER SOLUTION CLOUDY?

In hot weather, the sugar mixture may start to become cloudy. Improperly cleaned feeders can quicken the spoilage of the sugar mix, turning it cloudy. A mix that is too rich (contains too much sugar) can cloud up on cooler days.

Sometimes, the cheaper plastic feeders can begin to break down, with the plastic scratching after repeated cleanings and appearing cloudy.

HOW DO I STOP FINCHES AND ORIOLES FROM USING MY FEEDERS?

Once finches, orioles, or other birds learn that there is free dessert at these feeders, they will occasionally visit to satisfy their sweet tooth. However, they must use the perches on the feeders while stealing the hummingbirds' dinner, so buying feeders without perches is your best solution.

However, the perches are a valuable tool for weary hummingbirds to rest while feeding, as well. Therefore, you might consider moving the feeders with perches further away, while keeping the perchless feeders close so you can observe the hummingbirds.

HOW CAN I KEEP WASPS, HORNETS, BEES, AND ANTS AWAY FROM THE FEEDERS?

Hummingbirds will attack each other with ferocity, protecting more feeders than they could drain in an entire month. But, at the same time, they will (wisely) defer to smaller challengers like wasps.

Many feeders have insect guards built into the feeder. Still, these guards can become coated with syrup as the hummingbird feeds. However, if you keep the feeders clean and make sure they do not leak, you will reduce the appeal of the feeder to the insects.

Whatever you do, do not spray insecticide on or around the feeder to kill or repel insects.

If it is only bees that are intruding, consider adding a bee bath to your outdoor space. While ants and wasps are looking for sugar and can be deterred by keeping things clean, bees are usually only interested in staying hydrated.

Building your own bee bath is a simple project and lets you support another beneficial pollinator.

Why is there sugar solution on the deck below my feeder every day?

When birds (even hummingbirds) land on the feeder perches, the feeder swings, and some of the vacuum that holds the liquid in place may be broken, allowing spillage.

Despite their appearance as masters of flight, in complete control of their motion at all times, hummingbirds can be sloppy eaters. As they feed and insert or remove their beaks from the orifices, some of the sugar mix may adhere to their beaks, and droplets can spill. Since the heaviest feeding occurs at dusk and dawn, you will see more evidence of these lousy table manners in the morning.

Sugar-water will regularly end up below your feeders, so always consider what's below any possible feeder locations. However, syrup ending up on a deck does have one redeeming feature: it can attract gophers or the occasional squirrel, who lap up this dessert often.

The frequent spillage of sugar-water is another reason why you should clean your feeders every time you refill them.

Why do the hummingbirds seem to feed later in the morning in September?

There are a few reasons that hummingbirds feed later in the late summer and early autumn:

- If the nights are cool, the birds may have entered

torpor (a hibernation-like state that dramatically reduces their caloric needs at night) which takes a while to rouse from.
- The shorter days mean that the sun rises later and, without timepieces, the birds rely on the sun to awaken them. Cooler morning temperatures also mean that the birds are likely to wait longer to awaken.
- There are likely fewer birds around. Some may have begun migrating days or weeks earlier, so they may appear to arrive later because the activity level is lower.

How long will my feeder last?

Properly cared for, most moderately priced feeders will last four to six years with little maintenance.

Of course, you may want to occasionally touch up the accent colors or make sure that the feeding ports do not leak, but glass and HDPE plastics will last for several years.

If I repaint my feeder, will the paint harm the hummingbird?

Most commercial paints are listed as non-toxic. However, they still are chemical concoctions that should be used cautiously.

Select a paint labelled as 'no VOC' and ensure that it is completely dry and has not blocked any of the orifices in the feeder before returning it to use.

It is late in the season (or early in the season), and I have not seen any hummingbirds. How long should I leave my feeder out?

Put your feeders out a couple of weeks before you usually see hummingbirds arriving, and keep at least one feeder out for a couple of weeks after the last bird usually migrates.

Often, there are early arrivals and stragglers (much like people arriving too soon at parties or staying after they have worn out their welcome). Still, others may have been blown off course temporarily by storms. Late migrators have greater difficulty finding natural sources of food and may be in even greater need of a human benefactor to assist them.

The late season is a crucial time when humans need to keep their hummingbird feeders full. The supply of insects is dwindling, and most flowers have wilted and died. The feeders become the hummingbirds' emergency supplies as each bird hastens to develop the fat reserves it needs in order to make its southbound journey. The sugar-water may be pure calories with no nutrition, but calories create fat and establish reserves.

However, in late summer, nights can be cooler, and the liquid in the feeder can drop down to dangerous temperatures. Hummingbirds need to create fat and heat, not lose energy to cold sugar water. Therefore, many people take in their bird feeders overnight to keep them warm, putting them out very early in the morning. Don't worry – no hummingbirds feed at night, so you won't be starving anybody.

How can I stop my hummingbirds from fighting?

Hummingbirds – particularly male hummingbirds – are very territorial and fight to protect their feeding territory. This is a survival mechanism and cannot (and should not) be interfered with. For the first few days after fledging, male young will fight mock battles to establish a 'pecking order' but do not engage in serious attacks. Occasionally, immediately after mock fighting, the siblings may perch together to rest, then begin fighting again after a few minutes.

Even though hummingbirds can't walk or hop, when two hummingbirds 'square off' in mid air during defense of their feeding grounds, they drop their torsos and extend their legs, like kangaroos set to box. Some South American species even use their beaks to fence with other males. These encounters rarely result in serious injury, so sit back and enjoy the show!

I live on the eighth floor of an apartment. Would I be able to use a feeder to attract hummingbirds?

Hummingbirds feed below treetop level for the obvious reason that no flowers grow higher than that, so they are less likely to be willing to explore higher levels. Even when they migrate, the birds seldom fly above the treetops, so they can search for food while migrating and keep away from strong, buffeting winds.

However, some people have reported they have lured hummingbirds to their fifth- and sixth-floor windows, so it is possible to attract curious birds. As a general rule of thumb, if you live below the level of nearby treetops, there is potential for hummingbird visits.

WILL HUMMINGBIRDS BECOME DEPENDENT ON MY FEEDER SOLUTIONS?

Hummingbirds never rely entirely on your feeders, and this is a good thing in a couple of ways.

First, if people are inconsistent in putting out and maintaining feeders, like some are with songbird feeders, reliant hummingbirds would quickly starve.

Second, the sugar-water mixtures contain very few nutrients and lots of calories. The birds need the nutrients in plant nectar and about 10% of their diet as insect protein. They will naturally seek out flowers and insects in addition to the sugar solution.

Often, a bird at a feeder will flit back and forth between nearby flowers and the feeder, and they instinctively know to balance their diets.

PART III: FLOWERS

Even if our original motive in planting beautiful trees and flowers had nothing to do with attracting hummingbirds, simply planning the layout and introducing proper plants, trees, shrubs, and amenities will attract this adaptable little bird.

Backyard feeders are important to hummingbirds, but artificial feeding is only one component of a successful effort to provide a suitable environment for the hummingbird. More and more people are setting up comprehensive backyard habitats to accommodate the seasonal visitors. These include protected environments where they can shelter, as well as full-season natural foods and nesting areas.

As the modern world intrudes more and more into natural bird habitats, it becomes vital for the rest of us to provide the necessary spaces for wildlife. Many birds, from migratory birds like geese and ducks, crows, robins, and ruby-throated hummingbirds have found that they can live comfortably around humans. This bodes well for their long-term survival. Coyotes, raccoons, rabbits and even deer are also enjoying city gardens, where they have access to the minimal cover of brush and bush.

Interestingly, the deforestation of North America has not had a seriously negative impact on ruby. The flowering crops that replace trees, and the meadows that result from the open spaces and headlands edging the forests, provide more nectar and more insects.

On the other hand, the expansion of human population into rufous' territory has robbed him of valuable habitat. Ruby is increasing in population annually, while rufous' population has been decreasing since the 1960s. The loss of habitat is forcing the rufous to move into more marginal territory to find food, decreasing their survival rate.

Regardless of your opinion on these matters, you can always look at the green space you have created as a positive counterbalance, however small, to our society's impact on the natural world around us.

13

DESIGNING YOUR GARDEN

When starting on your design, it isn't about being pretty so much as it is about being functional. The layout and location are important, but so is the selection of plants and the timing of their growth and blooms. The inherent beauty of nature is how all components of ecological systems complement and support each other, filling all the necessary natural roles and existing in harmony with one another.

While there is always a strong temptation to put your own strong creative stamp on a space and exercise control over how your garden looks, creating a functional ecosystem will naturally bring about its own form of beauty and opportunities for appreciation.

Your backyard (or balcony) garden is the focal point for any hummingbirds that you will be able to entice. Still, it must be designed and carefully maintained so that you are not attracting predators, unwanted pests, or creating an unhealthy environment for your visitors. Size really does not matter. You will build within the limitations or expansiveness of the space available to you, applying established principles known to attract various hummingbirds.

Your planning should be guided by the goal of providing the basic requirements for your flying visitors. These requisites are safe feeding, safe nesting, and safe resting. As long as these elements are present and persist throughout the breeding season, you will be successful.

Most authorities suggest that hummingbirds are more attracted to color; however, there is evidence that they use shape to identify food as well. Artificial trees and plants draw in hummingbirds, who may attempt to drink nectar from lawn and garden ornaments. While hummingbirds are not shy about demonstrating their intelligence, even the brightest of us can get confused on occasion. Avoid introducing any flower-shaped decorations that could get mistaken for the real thing.

Begin with a sketch of your space. The key is how the garden is placed in relation to bushes, clearings, high traffic areas, and hazards. You should know:

- which plants will bloom at what times;
- which will attract the insects that hummingbirds consume;
- which plants will repel unwanted pests and deter predators; and
- which will be most attractive to the males as a stage for their courtship rituals.

Applying this knowledge well will make your garden a huge hit.

Many of the key plant species can thrive in pots or containers, and, as many apartment-dwelling hummingbird enthusiasts can attest, these small birds can still thrive in small spaces. Your garden will end up being both aesthetically pleasing and functional, blooming throughout the entire season and harboring as many hummingbirds as can tolerate each other.

The common element through all three basic needs is safety. Hummingbirds need to be able to flee from predators. It may seem intuitive that this extraordinarily agile and quick bird can escape any ground-bound predator, but that is not necessarily the case. The house cat is adept at stealth, and so fast that even a hummingbird can be caught unawares. Foxes, too, have been observed catching adult birds.

For this reason, your garden should have open space around it, like a meadow of mown grass, mimicking the forest clearings that hummingbirds naturally seek out. Predators hoping to catch the feeding birds by surprise will be more readily spotted as they creep across open areas between the fence, forest, or scrub outside your yard. Hummingbirds will only let down their guard to feed, rest, or nest when they have clear lines of sight around them.

At the same time, you do not want the feeders, food supply, and shelter exposed to perpetual sun. In addition, the flowers and plants that work best for hummingbird gardens need some shade.

Thus, it is important to allow for the growth of larger bushes or a few trees near the garden to act as shade and shelter. Vantage points where a bird can defend his feeding territory against intruder hummingbirds are also appreciated.

The ideal garden shape is long and relatively narrow. A narrow garden enables the bird to enter, feed, and quickly retreat if needed.

That doesn't mean that you are limited to building rectangular garden plots. Instead, consider shaping the garden in an arc or curve. This adds to the appeal of your backyard and more closely mimics stands of flowers in the wild that your hummingbirds would typically visit.

Having allotted the space and configuration for your garden, you can now plan the planting arrangement. Nature may seem random, but the most desirable plots in which different hummingbird species feed have elements in common that make those stands of flowers attractive to the feeding visitor.

14

THE FOUR ESSENTIALS

Those three basic needs for hummingbirds – safe feeding, safe nesting, and safe resting – are represented by four essential garden elements.

WATER

Even during preparations for migration, when hummingbirds should be at their busiest feeding, they will sit and enjoy a light drizzle of rain. Looking skyward with their wings slightly spread, they will catch raindrops while they fan their tail feathers.

While we watch as hummingbirds enjoy feeder upon feeder of nectar, we may think they do not require supplemental water. Yet, a supply of water is a vital component of a successful hummingbird backyard. There are a few ways that you can provide a proper supply of water.

First, hummingbirds love showers. They will often remain out in finely falling rain, occasionally fluffing and fluttering their wings to clean themselves. You can easily recreate this occurrence within your garden. Hummingbirds will fly back and forth through a misting feature or a simple garden sprinkler, taking detours between flowers, as long as the droplets are not too powerful.

If you have a misting system to cool off your human guests on hot days, consider extending it or adding another into a portion of your flower garden.

Decorative ponds or birdbaths with a misting feature are also ideal spots for the birds to shower. Generally, though, hummingbirds do not use standard-sized bird baths for bathing when shower facilities are available.

Shelter and Resting Areas

In between feedings, hummingbirds need to rest and digest. They do not have large stomachs, and their high metabolism requires quick injections of energy.

They also need vantage points from which they can spy on potential intruders. Of course, they also need places to rest at night if they are not on or in a nest.

As an extra cute option, hummingbirds seem to enjoy resting on tiny swings, which you can buy in pet stores.

Sitting Pretty — Example of a hummingbird swing

Nesting

Since hummingbirds do not like to feel closed in and will not nest in cavities or artificial birdhouses, it is counterproductive to place these devices in a hummingbird garden. In fact, it can be damaging. But even though a hummingbird will not use a nesting box that you built, that does not mean you cannot create a very appealing nesting environment that will stimulate hummingbirds and other birds to nest in your backyard.

Birdhouses for songbirds are appealing but, as with songbird feeders, they should not be placed in the hummingbird garden or the areas chosen to attract hummingbirds to breed. The presence of songbirds attracts predators of those birds, who, being opportunistic, will also ravage hummingbird nests.

Bat houses also should not be hung near the hummingbird area. At night, bats, who can hunt by echolocation, will often kill hummingbirds at rest. When the hummingbirds are in nightly torpor, it takes them a little while to awaken fully. If they are resting in an exposed area, they will succumb to bats or owls who have detected them. Bats also compete with the hummingbird for insects, and can be their most dangerous rivals for all of their lives.

Purple martin houses invite the martins to feast on many of the same insects on which hummingbirds feed and should be built on poles some distance from the hummingbird garden.

With the popularity of backyard beekeeping, you may be tempted to bring in a hive or two of bees to help pollinate your flowers. But bees, particularly in the late-season feeding frenzy, may attack hummingbirds. Worse, the hornets and wasps that often attempt to take over beehives become aggressive in the late summer. Frequently, they threaten hummingbirds at their feeders or in their favorite flowers.

There are specific things that hummingbirds seek and need for nest building.

First and foremost is a safe, familiar, and convenient nesting site. As described in the 'Nesting' chapter, a downward-sloping branch of a tree is preferred, and depending on the species, a specific type of tree or arrangement of trees (see chapter on "North American Hummingbird Species" for habitat and breeding venues).

For the predominant species across the middle and eastern part of North America, the ruby-throated hummingbird, stands with pine or deciduous trees and shrubs where the female can build a nest five to fifteen feet off the ground are perfect.

However, hummingbirds can be opportunists when it comes to nesting material and sites. So leave a ball of dryer lint in the open, do not destroy spider webs unnecessarily, and allow some of your dandelions or thistles to form downy heads. Plant a fast-growing cottonwood nearby.

The hummingbird will nest in any safe area near a good food supply, so having a garden with shrubbery and trees close, but not too close, will entice the female to nest.

If you are planting vines or pole beans in the garden, use netting in some spots so that the hummingbird may choose to use the netting or line on which to build a nest.

FEEDING

Hummingbirds prefer flowers that are not too close to the ground. Given a choice between petunias growing as a border plant or petunias in a hanging basket, they will opt for the hanging basket. Given a choice between bright red scarlet runners that may be fourteen feet tall and a similarly colored sweet william or geranium, they will choose the scarlet runner. However, they will feed on any flower they have identified as nectar-rich.

To feed, they need to be able to access the flowers and feeders safely, and observe approaching predators or other hummingbirds who want to challenge their authority to claim the feeding site. Therefore, the flowers should be layered from the edge to the center of the garden in order of the height to which they grow.

There is another reason why the flowers should be planted according to height whenever possible. While we were playing the part of a chef earlier, now we're heading over to the marketing department.

Think of arranging your garden like a store. Your customer wants easy, unimpeded access to look at all of your products up close, and doesn't want to have to search around for the bestsellers. Remember, hummingbirds are mostly influenced by visual cues and are looking for efficiency, so having clusters of bright flowers together works best.

Put the shortest flowers at the outer edges, where they won't be blocked and it is clear there are no predators in hiding. Then gradually layer in taller and brighter flowers, with your most enticing, brightest red flowers deeper in your garden. There should be clear separation between flower heights, so hummingbirds have clear entry and escape routes to all of your store shelves.

You also don't want to be carrying the same stock all of the time. Choose plants that bloom at different times of the season to ensure there is always something available. Gardens should be designed so that there is a continual explosion of color and nectar in each height zone, from the start of the blooming season to the autumn (fall).

Remember that shopping is hard work. Adding nearby places to perch, as well as a mixture of sun and shady spots near a food source will make life easier for your new friends.

Some extra flourishes, like using curved edges for your beds, can increase the number of angles from which hummingbirds can approach. Feeders can also be used to complement flowers, and hanging them from poles can add another vertical element if tall flowers are not possible.

Staging

There is a fifth (slightly less important) element to consider when designing a hummingbird habitat. Still, if you have successfully incorporated the other four, the fifth should follow naturally. To nest, the female needs to breed, and in order to breed, she needs to select a mate. That translates into the need to have a prime stage on which the male can perform for her.

The ideal spot has a safe perching area for the female to sit and watch the male's performance, while the male needs an open space to conduct his dance and aerial acrobatics. In the early part of the season, most of the garden plants will not be of sufficient size for her to perch, but if you have nearby shrubbery or trees, she will have an adequate grandstand. The space between the tree line and the garden will become a stage for males.

15

PLANT SELECTION

Hummingbirds have no sense of smell, but they see in vivid color, including the ultraviolet light spectrum. Many flowering plants that rely on insects to pollinate them contain ultraviolet-absorbing pigments in their petals, which are invisible to us but quickly catch the hummingbird's sensitive eyes.

Plants for a hummingbird garden are not the same as plants for a decorative garden or one to attract songbirds. That is because songbirds are seed eaters, whereas hummingbirds are nectar feeders.

Additionally, the flowers that attract bees and butterflies are not always the same flowers that attract hummingbirds. The hummingbird is not after seeds or even pollen. It is only interested in two food sources in your garden: small insects and nectar, and not all flowers produce enough nectar or nectar that is accessible.

One key benefit of providing plants as well as feeders is that while hummingbirds tend to be highly territorial and protective of 'their' feeder, they are more often willing to share access to flowers, allowing more hummingbirds unchallenged access to your outdoor space.

Use the following section as an initial starting point in selecting plants and flowers to fill out your garden design.

Try and choose native plants whenever possible for your garden, as these are the flowers with which the hummingbirds of the area are most familiar.

Hummingbirds' long beaks are ideal for reaching into the depths of tubular plants, which also tend to be the plants with the most nectar in the bowl of the flower and which have the least pollen.

As a general rule, the best plants are those that have flowers with long necks (such as morning glories) or tight mouth openings (such as scarlet runners), with bright red colours.

PLANT SELECTION

Recommended Hummingbird Flowers

Plant	Hardiness Zone	Height (feet)	Colour	Bloom Time
Bee Balm	4 - 9	2.5 - 4	Pink, red	Jul - Aug
Blazing Star	5 - 9	1 - 4	White	Jun - Aug
Bleeding heart	3 - 9	0.5 - 3	Rose, red	May - Jun
Bugleweed (wild)	3 - 9	1	Purple, blue	May - Jun
Cardinal flower	3 - 9	2 - 4	Red	Jul - Aug
Coral bells (some wild)	4 - 9	1 - 1.5	Red, rose	Jun - Sep
Columbine (some wild)	3 - 8	1 - 2	Red, yellow	May - Jun
Dahlia	3 - 9	3 - 4	Red, pink	Jul - Oct
Day lilies	3 - 9	1 - 6	Varied, red	Jun - Aug
Delphinium	3 - 9	3 - 8	Red, light blue	Jul - Aug
Fireweed (wild)	2 - 8	4 - 6	Red	Jun - Aug
Fuschia	4 - 9	1 - 10	Red	Jul - Aug
Gladiola	3 - 9	2 - 5	Varied	Jul - Sep
Hollyhock	3 - 9	6 - 8	Varied, red	May - July
Lily, Tiger (wild)	2 - 9	1 - 3	Red	Jul - Aug
Lily, Canada	3 - 9	2 - 5	Yellow	Jun - Jul
Lungwort	3 - 8	0.5 - 1	Pink, purple	Apr - May
Lupine	3 - 9	3 - 4	Purple	May - Jul
Nasturtium	2 - 9	1 - 10	Orange	Jun - Oct
Penstemon	3 - 8	1 - 9	Varied	Jun - Jul
Petunia	3 - 9	0.5 - 2	Varied	May - Oct
Phlox	3 - 9	2 - 4	Varied	Jul - Oct
Sage / Salvia	2 - 9	2 - 3	Red, purple	Jun - Jul
Snapdragon	3 - 9	2.5 - 4	Varied	Jun - Aug
Sweet William	3 - 9	1 - 3	Red, dark red	May - Jun
Zinnias	3 - 9	1 - 4	Varied	Jul - Oct

Recommended Hummingbird Vines and Trees

Plant	Hardiness Zone	Height (feet)	Colour	Bloom Time
Apple or Crabapple	4 - 7	5 - 10	White	Apr - May
Clematis	4 - 9	6 - 12	Varied	Apr - Aug
Dogwood	3 - 8	6 - 12	White	Apr - May
Hawthorne	3 - 9	15 - 30	White	Apr - May
Honeysuckle	3 - 9	up to 30	Yellow, red	Jun - Aug
Morning glory	4 - 9	6 - 10	Red, blue	Jul - Sep
Scarlet runner	2 - 9	up to 10	Red, orange	Jul - Oct
Trumpet vine	4 - 9	up to 30	Orange	Jul - Sep

Consider planting dwarf or ornamental trees or vines in or near your garden to act as shelter and perches for hummingbirds. Crab apple, mock orange, and mock apple are great additions. While the prospect of planting trees on a balcony may seem impossible, there are several variations of 'dwarf' tree species that grow perfectly well in larger pots or containers. Red buckeye, golden currant, and mountain laurel are great mid-height plants on which the birds can rest if you have a smaller space available.

Hummingbirds and bees are two of the most common pollinators in North America, but they don't have the same preferences. In general, flowers pollinated by bees are blue or purple, and have wide enough openings for bees to comfortably enter and gather pollen, with a handy landing/takeoff pad. Flowers pollinated by hummingbirds are typically a shade of red, with narrower openings that block access to everything but the hummingbirds' narrow bills.

Plants to Avoid

Rhododendrons may attract hummingbirds, but they are not very nectar-rich and, therefore, are not ideal for hummingbird gardens. Similarly, impatiens offer little nectar. Generally, flowers that rely on scent to attract pollinators are less likely to have abundant nectar and may have more pollen instead, such as marigolds, hydrangeas, and azaleas. However, these last two attract thousands of small gnats, aphids, and insects, which the hummingbirds need in their diets. Therefore, hydrangeas and azaleas are great supplemental plants to include in your hummingbird garden.

Other common flowers that hummingbirds generally avoid include: crocuses, daffodils, dianthus, forget-me-nots, gardenias, irises, lilacs, lily of the valley, marigolds, Oriental lilies, peonies, roses, sunflowers, sweet peas, and tulips.

Nesting & Sheltering

Hummingbirds want a feeding area close to their nesting areas, and both areas must be safe sites.

Where you plant trees, shrubs, fast-growing vines, and build shelters like trellises will determine whether or not your guests decide the site is safe. Larger trees can be outside the garden, perhaps at the outer edge of the clearing. Use trellises to support vines in the center of the garden, where the tallest plants will grow. These also provide a perch area for the hummingbirds.

Remember that your garden should either be further than thirty feet from windows and reflective surfaces or adjacent to them. This will prevent hummingbirds from flying at full speed as they approach these hazards.

The easier it is for your birds to thrive in your yard, the more likely they will take up permanent seasonal residence. That includes making sure that there are abundant natural and artificial materials for nest building.

Do not destroy spider webs during the breeding season. While the hummingbirds do not feed on the larger spiders, they do use the web material in every nest. Let dandelions bloom and form heads of fluff for the nests at the edges of the brush line on the outside of your garden. Put out your dryer lint, bits of thread and even balls of pet fur for the birds to use.

Birds that do not have to search far to find good nest material will be able to breed more rapidly, thus increasing your hummingbird population for next year.

16

MAINTENANCE & SAFETY

Maintaining your garden should not require excessive amounts of time. Hummingbirds care little about pruning, shaping, or weeding and prefer something a bit more 'wild' looking. Therefore, only basic care is required to keep your garden in appealing condition for you and the birds.

Instead of using commercial fertilizers, use compost from your kitchen or natural manures to enhance the soil and keep it rich, so abundant flowers are produced. In commercial fertilizers, the three primary ingredients are nitrogen, phosphorus, and potassium. Nitrogen stimulates the growth of leaves, while potassium and phosphorus promote the growth of fruit, roots, and flowers. Nitrogen occurs naturally at high levels in manure. Soil amendments like eggshells (for calcium), firewood ash, and banana peels are rich in flower-producing supplements. Use bone meal and other organic products if you rely on store-bought amendments.

Consider adding wild plants like milkweed at the fringes of your yard to attract butterflies and other insects. These insects help pollinate flowers before the hummingbirds arrive. Hummingbirds also use milkweed as a source of nectar.

Make sure that you deadhead flowers regularly. Plants like petunias require almost daily removal of the dying flowers. Once a plant produces seed, it generally starts dying, since its only function is to grow more plants. You can delay this process by a month or so by deadheading to keep blooms fresh and the plants vigorous.

Consider setting out overripe fruit, like bananas, at the far reaches of your garden to attract fruit flies, on which hummingbirds feast.

Many areas of North America are being invaded, not by people, but by plants. There are many invasive plants you should avoid and eradicate as they occur. Contact your local environmental groups or government agencies for help identifying any common invasive species. Do your best to ensure they haven't gotten a foothold in your hummingbird garden.

Avoid planting exotic flowering plants like Japanese honeysuckle. While hummingbirds love them, they will quickly crowd out local growth in fields and woodlands.

The purple loosestrife may seem appealing, but is a poor substitute for the flowers that it chokes out as it spreads across the continent. The dandelion – a European flower – has become a weed that crowds out other meadow plants, sucking up sparse moisture but offering little nectar to a hummingbird.

Other potentially invasive plant species to be wary of include: garlic mustard, giant hogweed, leafy spurge, autumn olive, common tansy, Canada thistle, European buckthorn, Japanese barberry, Scotch broom, salt cedar, and yellow iris.

You may have the urge to spray pesticides to remove insects whenever they become an excessive annoyance. But this can be hazardous and even deadly for the hummingbird, especially if not carefully planned and timed. Opting for natural treatments will minimize the risk to hummingbirds.

Several cities and municipalities across North America have adopted a natural approach to mosquito control. They have 'seeded' key areas with dragonfly larvae. These are voracious mosquito eaters and are harmless to all your plants (and even humans). Your local pest control company may be able to help you with your own program, or you can turn to butterfly conservation groups in the area for information.

Mosquitoes are very difficult to ignore, though. Use zappers where possible. Sprays can linger for a long time afterward, and are especially dangerous to the hummingbird. Insecticides disrupt the nervous system of insects, so it stands to reason that it could also affect small birds. Smokers are useful at night to keep mosquitoes at bay, and are less hazardous to the hummingbirds, since they are at rest in the bushes.

Particularly avoid pesticides and herbicides around the flower garden. Even a tiny amount of chemical that gets into the plant can also end up in the nectar, causing long-term damage to your birds. If they are absolutely necessary, time your chemical treatments to avoid prime feeding times of hummingbirds or when the dew is on the leaves and the birds are bathing in the moisture. Hummingbirds can also ingest poison when they eat insects that have been exposed. Hopefully, your hummingbirds are already hard at work catching small insects for you, while birds like swallows catch the larger ones, so there is no need for these products.

Keeping Hummingbirds Safe

By keeping the lawn short in the buffer zone between your garden and the boundaries of the yard, you enable the birds to see approaching stealth predators like squirrels, weasels, and, especially, cats.

The idea that a housecat is a risk to a hummingbird may seem somewhat far-fetched and is sure to cause push-back from devoted cat owners. Still, cats do indeed pose a threat to hummingbirds.

Yes, hummingbirds are quick – the best aerialists in the bird world. However, they hover in gardens with low-growing flowers and lots of camouflage cover for predators. It takes a fraction of a second for a cat to pounce, resulting in the loss of another hummingbird. It almost seems unfair to lure them into our urban gardens, only to have them act as prey for a housecat.

We can take measures to reduce the risk to the hummingbird. By applying natural deterrents for cats in the garden, using netting that frustrates cats, and by keeping cats indoors during the heaviest feeding times of early morning and late evening, you can minimize the risk to hummingbirds. Try to develop an environment that discourages feral cats by making sure there is nothing to attract vermin. You can ensure your garden does not attract cats by not leaving food or waste out that the cat can access. This includes secure garbage cans. You can also work with your local animal authority to trap feral cats.

Other birds can also pose a danger to hummingbirds, as smaller birds of prey like falcons, hawks, and merlins occasionally hunt them. Birds that frequently encounter predators will quickly start avoiding that area.

Even praying mantises in the southern USA and in Central and South America will capture and consume smaller hummingbirds. Smaller species like the bee hummingbird can also easily be caught in a spider web.

17

RISKS TO HUMMINGBIRDS

A conventional argument is that the most delicate members of an ecosystem, from frogs to insects to exotic plants, should be the first to be affected by changes in our climate and environment. However, the recent history of North America's hummingbird shows that what may appear delicate is often very resilient and adaptable.

For instance, because of their extremely high metabolism, hummingbirds are very susceptible to cold temperatures. They were originally tropical creatures after all. Yet, they now are found wintering in British Columbia rather than Columbia, South America. Where arid and non-arable land once existed, hummingbirds have intruded; their territories have expanded into the deserts of Nevada and the mountainsides of Washington State.

While, around the world, natural habitats for flora and fauna are being destroyed, manufactured structures and environments are stimulating the immigration of tiny animals like the hummingbird.

How we modify our own spaces can assist some wildlife in finding new homes if we plan correctly. Even though there are many risks to hummingbirds, there are also many solutions and easy actions that we can take to provide a healthier environment for them and all of the wild world around us.

There are several wildlife conservation groups, and even hummingbird-specific groups, that you can join or support. Often, in more broad conservation groups, you can be invited to form your own sub-group to focus on an area of concern that appeals to you. These can be a great opportunity not only to focus on conservation efforts but to get outdoors with like-minded people and explore the eco-systems around you.

The following are links to various hummingbird organizations, conservation groups, and protection initiatives in the United States and Canada.

American Bird Conservancy
https://abcbirds.org/ – is a registered non-profit dedicated to conserving wild birds and their habitats throughout the Americas.

Cornell Lab of Ornithology
https://www.birds.cornell.edu/home/ – is a research group that publishes information on birds for any level of interest, from beginners to dedicated researchers.

eBird
https://ebird.org/home – is an app from The Cornell Lab of Ornithology that identifies bird hotspots, and also lets you contribute any sightings to a global tracker.

Hummingbird Conservation Networks
https://www.savehummingbirds.org/ – monitors and studies hummingbird populations to support conservation. Their goal is to help hummingbirds survive, reproduce, and thrive while engaging human communities to demonstrate how they can benefit economically, socially, and ecologically through their hummingbird conservation activities.

Hummingbird Research, Inc.
http://hummingbirdresearch.net/ – is a 501(c)(3) nonprofit organization founded in 2009 by Fred Bassett to promote the conservation of hummingbirds through research and education. This group coordinates banding of hummingbirds to track populations and support research.

Hummingbirds Canada
http://hummingbirdscanada.ca/reportSighting – add your own sightings in Canada to this user-created map. This organization also bands hummingbirds to support research and conservation efforts.

International Ornithological Congress
https://www.internationalornithology.org/ – is an international group that seeks to support, promote, and advance avian biology.

National Audubon Society
https://www.audubon.org/ – is a science advocacy group that protects birds and the places they need, today and tomorrow, throughout the Americas, using education and on-the-ground conservation efforts.

Operation RubyThroat: The Hummingbird Project
http://www.rubythroat.org/default2.html – is an international cross-disciplinary initiative to the ruby-throated hummingbird. Although K-12 teachers and students are the primary target audience, Operation Ruby-Throat is open to anyone interested in hummingbirds.

Partners in Flight
https://partnersinflight.org/ – is a network of more than 150 partner organizations distributed throughout the Western Hemisphere. They are engaged in all aspects of landbird conservation including science, research, planning, and policy development.

RPBO Hummingbird Project
http://www.rpbo.org/hummingbirds.php – is a science-based project dedicated to the conservation of hummingbird populations and their habitats throughout British Columbia.

The Hummingbird Project
https://www.hummingbirdproject.org/ – is a non-profit that operates a number of initiatives domestically and globally in an effort to promote and educate communities about ecological regeneration.

The Hummingbird Society
http://www.hummingbirdsociety.org/index.php – is a non-profit organization that provides resources for hummingbird information, with a focus on protection of endangered species.

Western Hummingbird Partnership
https://westernhummingbird.org/ – is a clearinghouse for information relative to hummingbirds and hummingbird conservations.

18

PHOTOGRAPHY QUICK GUIDE

Inevitably, you will want to start snapping photos of your hummingbird friends to show off to others, or appreciate yourself later. Your smartphone is probably more than sufficient to get some impressive shots. But here are some tips if you want to take things a step further, or if you use a traditional camera.

First off, take your time and be deliberate. You aren't hiding out in a camouflaged hut in the jungle, waiting for a once-in-a-lifetime opportunity. Be patient and avoid the temptation to take hundreds of rapid-fire photos. You'll need to spend hours going through them later.

Also, remember to make sure you're not missing great moments while organizing your photos! As you become more familiar with hummingbirds, you will start recognizing their behaviors, patterns, and personalities, hopefully getting ideas of the action you want to capture and when and where it might happen.

Along with your growing understanding of hummingbirds, they will become more comfortable with you. Most wild animals instinctively know how close they can let a predator (or unfamiliar human) get before they have to flee. As you approach this invisible boundary, birds will become more and more cautious, and if you cross the line, they will feel pressured to make an escape.

However, if you are the person who has been refilling their feeder all summer, or have at least spent a few weeks blending in with the scenery, the invisible boundary might begin to shrink. But even if it doesn't, you can learn just how much personal space you need to give each hummingbird to get your award-winning photos.

A general rule of thumb is that the action around the feeders will be busiest in the morning and evening, which is also the time of day with the best lighting for photos. Since you have some degree of control over your 'photography studio', make sure that you are avoiding setting up shots in shadows, harsh light, or with distracting backgrounds.

Hummingbirds might allow you to get right next to them, which sounds great in theory, but that position might put your subjects closer than the minimum focusing distance of your camera lens. This minimum distance can range from seven to nine feet (2.2 to 2.8 m) for 150-600 mm and 200-600 mm camera lenses. Based on the type of lens you have, find the ideal distance for your camera to properly focus, position your back towards the sun, and shoot away.

When it comes to your camera settings, a good place to start for beginner photographers is to put your camera in manual mode with auto ISO. How to do this will depend on the model of your camera; so unfortunately, you will need to read the manual.

ISO controls how much light your camera allows to reach the sensor. Letting your camera automatically control this element enables you to focus on the two other key components of photography: aperture and shutter speed.

The aperture setting separates your subject from the background and adjusts the depth of field of your photos. The best setting will depend on your camera, but a half-stop above the widest setting is a great place to start. So if your camera's maximum aperture is f/5, start at f/5.5.

Play around with your aperture setting at different points in your outdoor space, and see which settings give you the best feel. You can practice by focusing on a specific flower your hummingbirds love or your feeder to see what works best.

For shutter speed, the key consideration is how fast your subject is moving. For example, a hummingbird resting on a perch might not need a fast shutter speed, but if you are trying to capture a crisp vision of a hummingbird in flight, you will need something much faster, ideally above 1/2000s. Lower shutter speeds will result in motion blur, which can be a neat artistic effect.

If you have a tripod and want a high-quality image of a resting hummingbird, a slower shutter speed between 1/250 and 1/800 will be very effective. If your camera doesn't have an auto ISO setting, you might notice your shutter speed slowing under lower light conditions. If that happens, manually increase your ISO until it stops limiting your shutter speed.

Some less critical settings to consider when fine-tuning your photography are frame-release and autofocus. Set your frame release as high as possible if you are taking bursts of images. For focus, try using a single autofocus point and aim at the hummingbird's head. If your subject refuses to stay in one place, a dynamic focus setting might work better. Just make sure there aren't any other potential focus points (like branches or shadows) in the background

Another fantastic option is to set up motion-activated cameras, or video feeds. You never know what wildlife might get up to when they think nobody is watching.

Again, you will want to learn how your hummingbirds use your outdoor space first, so you know what behaviors you wish to capture. Then you can decide on the best angles to photograph or film those moments and where to place the equipment.

CONCLUSION

We all crave a connection with nature that makes us feel like we are an integral part of the wild world around us.

And now that you know the story of hummingbirds, it's time for you to get out there and put all of this knowledge to good use. There are always new details to discover, and things to experience which can't really be fully appreciated by just reading about them.

If you enjoyed 'Attracting Hummingbirds' please don't be shy about saying so! My goal is to help as many people as possible appreciate the environment around us, so feel free to share this book with your friends and family (and please leave a review at your preferred retailer).

Whether you will appreciate them from afar, set-up a simple feeder on a balcony, or build your own backyard oasis, I hope this is just the beginning of you creating your own unique stories about hummingbirds.

DON'T FORGET YOUR FREE GIFT

Use my **'Outdoor Space Planner'** to:

- Get inspired, and choose what elements you *like*, *want*, or *need* to have in your new outdoor space
- Identify any special requirements or restrictions that might be roadblocks to improving your backyard or balcony
- Create an easy to follow budget so you don't run out of money, space, or time
- Draw out your personalized design and plan a schedule for everything to get delivered, built, and installed.

Go to https://www.subscribepage.com/danielistein to get it now!

NORTH AMERICAN HUMMINGBIRD SPECIES

There are twenty-four species of hummingbirds that either live in, migrate to, or occasionally visit North America. Many are found only in the southeastern US states, bordering the Gulf of Mexico, or in the southwestern US.

The following section summarizes the physical description, habitat, and seasonal territories of each bird. In addition, the conservation status of each bird is listed. Take note that none of the species of hummingbirds, to date, are listed in the 'threatened' or 'endangered' categories. Still, some have declining populations, primarily due to habitat loss.

If you are trying to figure just who is visiting your feeders or flowers, here are some basic tips when trying to identify hummingbird species:

- Colors – these can be hard to confirm on juveniles and females, especially when the birds are moving

around quickly, but if you manage to get a picture you can check the coloring on their back, head (crown, cap, or face), gorget (throat), underparts, wings, and bill.
- Trying to tell males from females can be tricky for some species. Usually only males will have colorful iridescent feathers, and they will be the ones showing off with louder chirps, a stronger humming sound, and aggressively defending their territory while performing dives. Females may have white tips or spots on their tails, are usually noticeably larger than males, sometimes up to 25 percent bigger, and may be spotted gathering nesting materials. Juvenile hummingbirds tend to look like smaller versions of the females.
- Check their geographic range, because some similar-looking species might not share the same territory.
- If all else fails, try using the Merlin bird identification app, which you can get from the Cornell Lab of Ornithology.

Allen's Hummingbird

Selasphorus sasin

Habitat: Found on the Pacific coast (California, Oregon, Washington, British Columbia). Prefer brushy woods and fields, and are common in backyard gardens. Winter in Central America and Mexico.

Distinguishing features: Copper or green back, orange flanks and tail, long straight bill. Males have an orange throat with a white crescent underneath and pointy tail feathers. Females have an orange-red spotty throat.

Conservation status: Least concern.

Notes: Year-round residents of southwest California. Females are often mistaken for rufous hummingbirds.

Anna's Hummingbird

Calypte anna

Habitat: West coast of US and Canada and do not migrate. Prefer open areas near water, but will commonly feed and nest in backyards.

Distinguishing features: Smaller hummingbirds, iridescent bronzy-green back, dull green underparts, green sides, grey chest, straight black bill. Males have a pink to crimson gorget and cap. Females have white ends on their tails and paler undersides.

Conservation status: Not endangered.

Notes: Hybridize with Costa's. Tend to hold their tails still while feeding.

Antillean Crested Hummingbird

Orthorhyncus cryostats

Habitat: Vagrant species in Florida. Native to the Caribbean but have recently been sighted breeding in Florida. Prefer moist tropical forest borders.

Distinguishing features: Green crest, purple and green colored body, short black bill.

Conservation status: Least concern.

Notes: Not native to the US.

Bahama Woodstar

Nesophlox evelynae

Habitat: Native to the Bahamas, but occasionally spotted in the Florida Keys. Prefer gardens, scrubland, and edges of tropical evergreen growth. Do not migrate.

Distinguishing features: Green and gold back, olive buff underparts. Males have purple gorgets and white flanks. Females are more cinnamon colored.

Conservation status: Least concern.

Notes: Not native to the US. Very unsociable.

Berylline Hummingbird

Amazilia beryllina

Habitat: Southwestern Arizona and west Texas, winter in central America. Prefer oak forests near streams.

Distinguishing features: Mostly metallic green, light green gorget, orange-rust wings and tail, straight bill with black on top and red below. Females are less colorful than males.

Conservation status: Least concern.

Notes: Do not typically nest in the USA, but will aggressively defend feeders.

Black-Chinned Hummingbird

Archilochus alexandri

Habitat: Western US and Canada, as far east as Utah, Nevada, and Texas. Very adaptable and live in urban and wild habitats. Prefer open locations near water. Winter in Mexico, but occasionally seen in California.

Distinguishing features: Metallic green back, white underbelly, long, black, straight bills, and forked tail. Males have a black face and dark purple throat that can appear black in low light conditions. Females appear similar to ruby-throats with white tips on their tail feathers and a white throat.

Conservation status: Least concern.

Notes: Hybridize with Anna's, lucifer, broad-billed, and Costa's hummingbirds. Not very territorial; will move and fan their tails while feeding.

Blue-Throated Mountain-Gem

Lampornis clemenciae

Habitat: Southwestern US (Arizona, New Mexico, Texas). Prefer wooded canyons and forested areas, but will occasionally visit feeders. Winter in southern Arizona and Mexico.

Distinguishing features: Largest North American hummingbirds, dull green or bronze upper parts, grey under parts, white stripe behind eye, black tails with large white tips, straight black bill. Males have an iridescent blue gorget.

Conservation status: Least concern.

Notes: Rare. Also known as the blue-throated hummingbird.

Broad-Billed Hummingbird

Cynanthus latirostris

Habitat: Southern Arizona and New Mexico, but have recently been spotted in Oregon, Idaho, and Colorado. Prefer streamside groves, oak woodlands, and dense vegetation but will visit feeders. Winter in Mexico and Baja California.

Distinguishing features: Metallic-green back, slightly forked tail, straight red bill with black tip. Males have a blue gorget that extends to their breast and a blackish-blue tail. Females have a pale belly and a white stripe behind the eye.

Conservation status: Least Concern

Notes: They will wag their tails while hovering and feeding. Similar appearance to magnificent (Rivoli's) hummingbirds.

Broad-Tailed Hummingbird

Selasphorus platycercus

Habitat: Western US and Canada mountains, except for the Pacific Coast. Winter in Guatemala and Mexico, but a large portion of the population does not migrate north. Prefer pine and oak trees for nesting at 5,000 - 10,000 feet elevation, and forage in open areas. Will regularly visit feeders while migrating.

Distinguishing features: Iridescent green back, brownish wings, white chin and eye patches, round black tail, and straight black bill. Males have red throats with dark, notched tails edged with red. Females have cinnamon flanks and spotted cheeks, with a bicolored tail that has white tips.

Conservation status: Least concern.

Notes: Distinctive 'zinging' sound of wings during flight, much louder than other hummingbirds.

Buff-Bellied Hummingbird

Amazilia yucatanensis

Habitat: South Texas, extending along the Gulf Coast to the Florida panhandle in winter. Prefer forests and thickets and pine or oak forests, and are also found in orchards and citrus groves. Winter in Belize and Guatemala.

Distinguishing features: Metallic-green backs and heads, buff-colored lower breasts, long, rounded, rust-red tail, curved red bill with black tip. Males have a golden or green-black gorget.

Conservation status: Least concern.

Notes: Appear similar to Berylline hummingbird, but their ranges do not overlap.

Cinnamon Hummingbird

Amazilia rutila

Habitat: South Arizona and Texas. Prefer subtropical or tropical dry biomes first. Winter in Mexico, Belize, Panama, and Costa Rica.

Distinguishing features: Metallic bronze-green back, dark green wings, cinnamon stomach from chin to tail, red bill with black tip.

Conservation status: Least concern.

Notes: Only recently observed in the southwestern USA.

Calliope Hummingbird

Stellula calliope

Habitat: Pacific northwest and interior of the US (Oregon, Washington, Montana, Colorado, Arizona, New Mexico) and Canada (British Columbia). Prefer low flowers and higher perching positions, and nesting in evergreen trees.

Distinguishing features: Smallest North American hummingbirds, glossy green back and crown, white underparts, black tail, straight black bill. Males have pink-magenta streaks on their gorget that extends to points, and a pale face. Females have white tips on their tails and a pinkish tinge on sides.

Conservation status: Least concern.

Notes: Migrate early, arriving in mid-April or early May. Less aggressive than and easily intimidated by other hummingbirds.

Costa's Hummingbird

Calypte costae

Habitat: Found on the Pacific coast and in the southwestern US (Arizona, New Mexico, Nevada, Utah, Texas, California, northwest Mexico). Prefer brushy desert or arid areas, and winter in Mexico or southeastern California. Uncommon in backyards.

Distinguishing features: Grayish or green back and sides, white breast and underbelly, and a straight black bill. Males have an iridescent purple crown and gorget, ending in flared points. Smaller than most hummingbirds, at only 3 - 3.5 inches (7.5 - 8.9 cm) long.

Conservation status: Least concern.

Notes: Hybridize with the black-chinned hummingbird.

Cuban Emerald

Riccordia ricordii

Habitat: Florida and Florida Keys. Prefer semi-open subtropical habitats. Non-migratory and native to the Bahamas and Cuba.

Distinguishing features: Iridescent green color, white spot behind the eye. Females have grey throat, breast, and belly.

Conservation status: Least concern.

Notes: Not seen in North America until recently.

Green-Breasted Mango

Anthracothorax prevostii

Habitat: South Texas along the Gulf Coast. Prefer deciduous forests, open fields, orchards, and gardens. Partially migratory, and usually remain in Venezuela, Columbia, Peru, and Ecuador.

Distinguishing features: Glossy green upper parts, bright green flanks, dark blue or black chest and underparts, black stripe on throat, reddish purple tail, long, curved, black bill. Males have green gorgets. Females have white tips on the tail and occasionally magenta outer tail feathers, and white underparts.

Conservation status: Least concern (recommended for 'nearly threatened' status)

Notes: Rare; historically only found in the tropics.

Green Violet-Ear Hummingbird

Colibri thalassinus

Habitat: South and central Texas. Prefer temperate forests and high-altitude areas. Winter in southern Mexico. Known to wander and have rarely been seen as far north as Canada.

Distinguishing features: Glittering violet triangular ear patch, shiny green back, bright green throat, blue-green tail, straight black bill. Males and females appear similar, but females have duller colors.

Conservation status: Least concern.

Notes: Rarely breed in the USA; aggressive behavior at feeders. Also know as the Mexican violet-ear hummingbird.

Lucifer Sheartail

Calothorax lucifer

Habitat: West Texas, southeastern Arizona, and southwestern New Mexico. Prefer desert canyons, and dry washes with shrubbery at altitudes of 3,000 - 5,500 feet. Winter in central Mexico.

Distinguishing features: Green upperparts, forked tail, downward-curved black bill. Males have a bright pink flared gorget and a white breast. Females have a grey ear-streak, with streaks of red at the base of the tail, and white tips on the end of the tail.

Conservation status: Least concern.

Notes: Rare, and do not visit backyards often. Nest on cacti. Also known as the lucifer hummingbird.

Plain Capped Star-Throat

Heliomaster constant

Habitat: Southern Arizona. May not migrate every year, and do not stray far north past Mexico. Prefer lower elevation areas of mountains, ravines, and dry gulches. Will use feeders.

Distinguishing features: Red-brown gorget, metallic bronze-black tail and crown, greyish-white breast and rump spot, dark grey and white eye stripes, slightly ridged tail, straight, long, black bill. Females have slightly duller colors.

Conservation status: Least concern.

Notes: Extremely rare. Coloring is generally dull.

Rivoli's Hummingbird

Eugenes fulgens

Habitat: Southwestern US (Arizona, New Mexico, eastern California, western Texas). Prefer ravines and open meadows near oak or pine forests.

Distinguishing features: Large hummingbirds, very dark green iridescent color, white spot behind the eye, straight, long, black bill. Males have a dark blue-green gorget, with a violet cap and crown. Females have greyish-white underparts.

Conservation status: Least concern.

Notes: Rare. Will visit feeders and can be aggressive. Also know as the magnificent hummingbird.

Ruby-Throated Hummingbird

Archilochus colubris

Habitat: Summer range extends across the central and eastern states of the USA, and from the Maritime provinces of Canada to Alberta. Occasionally seen in western British Columbia mountains. Prefer deciduous and pine forests but adapt well to urban environments. Winter in Central America, Mexico and southern portions of Florida.

Distinguishing features: Metallic green backs and crown, grey-white underparts, and a straight black bill. Males have metallic red gorgets bordered by a white collar, and slightly forked tails. Females have notched tails with white tips, with more brownish heads and sides and a spotted throat.

Conservation status: Least concern

Notes: The most common hummingbird to the east of the Mississippi. Males are aggressive and migrate south early (August).

Rufous Hummingbird

Selasphorus rufus

Habitat: Northern Pacific coast (Washington, Oregon, Idaho, British Columbia, Southern Alaska). Prefer mountain habitats at forest edges, and tubular alpine flowers. Winter in central Mexico, southern California, and some southeastern Gulf states. Rare in urban areas.

Distinguishing features: White breast, orange or rust-colored back, flanks, face, and tail, straight bill. Males have an orange-red gorget and upper parts, and some have a green cap. Females have less pronounced colors, might have a greenish tinge, and white tips on their tail. Appear similar to Allen's, but live further north.

Conservation status: Nearly threatened.

Notes: Very territorial and aggressive. If present, it is recommended to space feeders apart as much as possible. They will likely chase off any other species.

Violet-Crowned Hummingbird

Amazilia violiceps

Habitat: Southeast Arizona and southwest New Mexico. Prefer low elevations or canyons near water, and sycamore trees.

Distinguishing features: White throat and breast with purple cap, grey-green upper body, white underparts, metallic blue-green tails, straight black bill with red tip. Males and females appear similar, but females are less colorful.

Conservation status: Least concern.

Notes: Rare.

White-Eared Hummingbird

Hylocharis leucotis

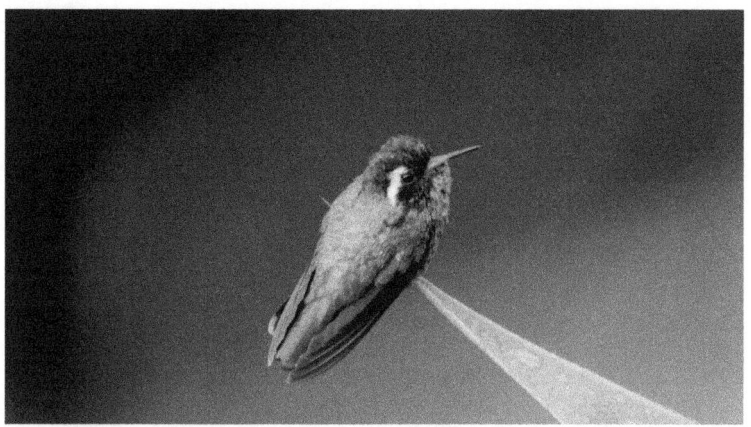

Habitat: Southwestern US (Arizona, Texas, New Mexico). Prefer pine-oak forests in mountains and canyons. Winter in Mexico and Nicaragua. Year-round resident of Arizona.

Distinguishing features: Green upperparts, paler dull underparts, bronzy green tail, white stripe between eye and ear, straight red bill with black tip. Males have turquoise gorgets, violet and black patches on their heads, and forked tails. Females have straight tails and lighter coloring.

Conservation status: Least concern

Notes: Aggressive at feeders. Will spread tail feathers while feeding.

Xantus Hummingbird

Hylocharis xantusii

Habitat: Southern California. Prefer meadows adjacent to wooded areas, and will readily visit gardens and feeders. Occasionally seen as far north as British Columbia.

Distinguishing features: Green colored backs, cinnamon underparts, rust-red tail, white eye stripe, straight red bill with black tip. Males have iridescent green gorget that can appear black.

Conservation status: Least concern.

Notes: Do not migrate, but will follow the blooming season. Very challenging to photograph.

IMAGE CREDITS

COVER AND INTRODUCTION

Cover and Introduction, Anna's Hummingbird (Calypte Anna), provided by Fireglo2, from Getty Images Pro, under the Canva One Design Use License Agreement.

Helping hand, provided by Ravina Chandra, used with permission.

Unique features, Sword-billed hummingbird image [Sword-billed Hummingbird RWD2.jpg], by DickDaniels, from commons.wikimedia.org, under the Creative Commons Attribution-Share Alike 3.0 license. Snowcap hummingbird image [Snowcap (Microchera albocoronata).jpg], by Michael Woodruff, under the Creative Commons Attribution-Share Alike 2.0 Generic license. Swallow-tailed hummingbird image [Eupetomena macroura -Piraju, São Paulo, Brazil-8.jpg], by Dario Sanches, from commons.wikimedia.org, under the Creative Commons Attribution-Share Alike 2.0 Generic license.

FLIGHTS

Rufous hummingbird, Male rufous image [hummingbird-5111260_960_720], by BlenderTimer, from pixabay.com, under the Pixabay License (free for commercial use, no attribution required). Female Rufous image [Rufous hummingbird female.jpg], by Sberardi, from commons.wikimedia.org, under the Creative Commons Attribution-Share Alike 3.0 Unported license.

Ruby-throated hummingbird, Male ruby-throated [Ruby-throated HummingBird.jpg], by Djgreene, from commons.wikimedia.org, under the Creative Commons Attribution-Share Alike 3.0 Unported license. Female Ruby-throated [Female Ruby-throated Hummingbird.jpg], by Pslawinski, from commons.wikimedia.org, under the Creative Commons Attribution-Share Alike 3.0 Unported license.

WINTER HOLIDAYS

Tough customer, Tooth-billed hummingbird [Androdon aequatorialis (Tooth-billed Hummingbird) (7162180046).jpg], by Andres Cuervo, from commons.wikimedia.org, under the Creative Commons Attribution-Share Alike 2.0 Generic license. Male and Female bills image from Rico-Guevara et al. 2019. Shifting Paradigms in the Mechanics of Nectar Extraction and Hummingbird Bill Morphology. Integrative Organismal Biology. 1(1): pp 1-15.

HEADING NORTH

Anna's hummingbird, Male Anna's [annas-hummingbird-5837675_960_720], by Veronica_Andrews, from pixabay.com, under the Pixabay License (free for commercial use, no attribution required). Female Anna's [annas-hummingbird-5821927_960_720], by bryanhanson1956, from pixabay.com, under the Pixabay License (free for commercial use, no attribution required).

West coast neighbors, Male Allen's hummingbird [Allen's Hummingbird (26724580157).jpg], by Becky Matsubara, from commons.wikimedia.org, under the Creative Commons Attribution 2.0 Generic license. Male Black-chinned hummingbird [Black-chinned Hummingbird, Arizona 04.jpg], by VJAnderson, from commons.wikimedia.org, under the Creative Commons Attribution-Share Alike 4.0 International license. Male Calliope hummingbird [Caliope hummingbird, Stellula calliope male, gorget.jpg], by Kati Fleming, from commons.wikimedia.org, under the Creative Commons Attribution-Share Alike 3.0 Unported license. Male Broad-tailed hummingbird [Broad-tailed Hummingbird Selasphorus platycercus; male perched on branch.jpg], by Kati Fleming, from commons.wikimedia.org, under the Creative Commons Attribution-Share Alike 3.0 Unported license.

Migration Roadmap, by Robert Lee, used with permission.

MATING SEASON

Ready to put on a show, Male Costa's hummingbird [Costa's hummingbird by Pete Gregoire (10127567666).jpg], by Pete Gregoire, from commons.wikimedia.org, under the Creative Commons Attribution 2.0 Generic license.

Letting her lead, Male blue-throated mountain gem [Blue-throated Hummingbird South Fork Cave Creek AZ 2015-07-01at11-18-138 (33930794408).jpg], by Bettina Arrigoni, from commons.wikimedia.org, under the Creative Commons Attribution 2.0 Generic license.

NESTING

Marvel of engineering, Female ruby-throated hummingbird [Ruby-throated hummingbird on nest 01.jpg], by Lorie Shaull, from commons.wikimedia.org, under the Creative

Commons Attribution-Share Alike 4.0 International license.

Light as a feather, Allen's hummingbird nest [Allen's Hummingbird Nest (8563916462).jpg], by Mike's Birds, from commons.wikimedia.org, under the Creative Commons Attribution-Share Alike 2.0 Generic license.

CHOOSING YOUR FEEDER

Vacuum feeder, provided by Sheldon Stein, used with permission.

Saucer feeder, image of hummingbird at saucer-style feeder [hummingbird-176882_960_720], by ev3177, from pixabay.com, under the Pixabay License (free for commercial use, no attribution required).

THE FOUR ESSENTIALS

Sitting Pretty, Copper beaded hummingbird swing, from www.wayfair.com.

NORTH AMERICAN HUMMINGBIRD SPECIES

Allen's, Left [allens-hummingbird-338671_960_720], by ArtTower, from pixabay.com, under the Pixabay License (free for commercial use, no attribution required). Right [Allen's Hummingbird (29139474635).jpg], by Mike's Birds, from commons.wikimedia.org, under the Creative Commons Attribution-Share Alike 2.0 Generic license.

Anna's, Left [annas-hummingbird-5837675_960_720], by Veronica_Andrews, from pixabay.com, under the Pixabay License (free for commercial use, no attribution required). Right [annas-hummingbird-5821927_960_720], by bryanhanson1956, from pixabay.com, under the Pixabay License (free for commercial use, no attribution required).

Antillean Crested, Male [Antillean crested hummingbird.jpg], by Charles J. Sharp, from commons.wikimedia.org, under the Creative Commons Attribution 3.0 Unported license.

Bahama Woodstar, [Bahama Woodstar - Calliphlox evelynae.jpg], by New Jersey Birds, from commons.wikimedia.org, under the Creative Commons Attribution-Share Alike 2.0 Generic license.

Berylline, [Berylline Hummingbird.jpg], by dominic sherony, from commons.wikimedia.org, under the Creative Commons Attribution-Share Alike 2.0 Generic license.

Black-chinned, Left [Black-chinned Hummingbird, Arizona 04.jpg], by VJAnderson, from commons.wikimedia.org, under the Creative Commons Attribution-Share Alike 4.0 International license. Right [Black-chinned Hummingbird, Arizona 02.jpg], by VJAnderson, from commons.wikimedia.org, under the Creative Commons Attribution-Share Alike 4.0 International license.

Blue-throated mountain gem, Left [Blue-throated Hummingbird South Fork Cave Creek AZ 2015-07-01at11-18-138 (33930794408).jpg], by Bettina Arrigoni, from commons.wikimedia.org, under the Creative Commons Attribution 2.0 Generic license. Right [Blue-throated Mountaingem, Cave Creek Canyon, Chiricahua Mts.jpg], by sloalan, from commons.wikimedia.org, under the Creative Commons CC0 1.0 Universal Public Domain Dedication.

Broad-billed, Left [BroadbilledHummingbird.jpg], by www.naturespicsonline.com, from commons.wikimedia.org, under the Creative Commons Attribution-Share Alike 3.0 Unported license. Right [Broad-billed Hummingbird. Cynanthus latirostris. Female - Flickr - gailhampshire.jpg], by gailhampshire, from commons.wikimedia.org, under the Creative Commons Attribution 2.0 Generic license.

Broad-tailed, Left [Broad-tailed Hummingbird Selasphorus platycercus; male perched on branch.jpg], by Kati Fleming, from commons.wikimedia.org, under the Creative Commons Attribution-Share Alike 3.0 Unported license. Right [Selasphorus platycercus1.jpg], by Bill Ratcliff, from commons.wikimedia.org, the image contains material based on a work of a National Park Service employee, created as part of that person's official duties. As a work of the U.S. federal government, such work is in the public domain in the United States.

Buff-bellied, Male [Buff-bellied Hummingbird Tex.jpg], by Tony Castro, from commons.wikimedia.org, under the Creative Commons Attribution-Share Alike 4.0 International license.

Cinnamon, Male [Cinnamon Hummingbird - Mexico S4E8524.jpg], by Francesco Varonesi, from commons.wikimedia.org, under the Creative Commons Attribution-Share Alike 2.0 Generic license. Right, [Cinnamon Hummingbird (Amazilia rutila)(cropped).jpg], by Dominic Sherry, from commons.wikimedia.org, under the Creative Commons Attribution-Share Alike 2.0 Generic licence.

Calliope, Right [Caliope hummingbird, Stellula calliope male, gorget.jpg], by Kati Fleming, from commons.wikimedia.org, under the Creative Commons Attribution-Share Alike 3.0 Unported license. Left [Immature male calliope Hummingbird 15.jpg], by HoustonRyan, from commons.wikimedia.org, under the Creative Commons Attribution-Share Alike 3.0 Unported license.

Costa's, Right [Costas-hummingbird.JPG], by K.lee, from commons.wikimedia.org, under the Creative Commons Attribution-Share Alike 3.0 Unported license. Left [Costas Hummingbird female RWD2.jpg], by Dick Daniels, under the Creative Commons Attribution-Share Alike 3.0 Unported license.

Cuban emerald, Right [cuba-3254001_960_720], by Barbee-Anne, from pixabay.com, under the Pixabay License (free for commercial use, no attribution required). Left [Cuban emerald (Chlorostilbon ricordii ricordii) female cr.jpg], by Charles J. Sharp, from commons.wikimedia.org, under the Creative Commons Attribution-Share Alike 4.0 International license.

Green-breasted mango, Male [Green-breasted Mango (Anthracothorax prevostii)RWD.jpg], by Dick Daniels, from commons.wikimedia.org, under the Creative Commons Attribution-Share Alike 3.0 Unported license.

Green violet-ear, Male [GreenVioletear.jpg], by Mmcnally, from commons.wikimedia.org, under the Creative Commons Attribution-Share Alike 3.0 Unported license.

Lucifer, Left [Lucifer Hummingbird - Flickr - gailhampshire.jpg], by gaiilhampshire, from commons.wikimedia.org, under the Creative Commons Attribution 2.0 Generic license. Right [Flickr - ggallice - Hummingbird.jpg], by Geoff Gallice, from commons.wikimedia.org, under the Creative Commons Attribution 2.0 Generic license.

Plain-capped starthroat, Unknown [hummingbird-4553235_960_720], by Akiroq, from pixabay.com, under the Pixabay License (free for commercial use, no attribution required).

Rivoli's, Left [Rivoli's Hummingbird, male (formerly Magnificent Hummingbird) 03.jpg], by VJAnderson, from commons.wikimedia.org, under the Creative Commons Attribution-Share Alike 4.0 International license. Right [Rivoli's Hummingbird, male (formerly Magnificent Hummingbird) 02.jpg], by VJAnderson, from commons.wikimedia.org, under the Creative Commons Attribution-Share Alike 4.0 International license.

Ruby-throated, Left [Ruby-throated HummingBird.jpg], by D jgreene, from commons.wikimedia.org, under the Creative Commons Attribution-Share Alike 3.0 Unported license. Right [Female Ruby-throated Hummingbird.jpg], by Pslawinski, from commons.wikimedia.org, under the Creative Commons Attribution-Share Alike 3.0 Unported license.

Rufous, Left [hummingbird-5111260_960_720], by Blender-Timer, from pixabay.com, under the Pixabay License (free for commercial use, no attribution required). Right [Rufous hummingbird female.jpg], by Sberardi, from commons.wikimedia.org, under the Creative Commons Attribution-Share Alike 3.0 Unported license.

Violet-crowned, Unknown [Violet-crowned Hummingbird, Arizona 03.jpg], by VJAnderson, from commons.wikimedia.org, under the Creative Commons Attribution-Share Alike 4.0 International license.

White-eared, Unknown [White-eared Hummingbird (Basilinna leucotis).jpg], by Dominic Sherony, from commons.wikimedia.org, under the Creative Commons Attribution-Share Alike 2.0 Generic license.

Xantus, Male [Hylocharis xantusii.jpg], by marlin harms, from commons.wikimedia.org, under the Creative Commons Attribution 2.0 Generic license.

Conclusion

Conclusion [cute-feeding-small-wildlife], by Anonymous, from pxfuel.com, under a free-for-commercial-use license.

ENDNOTES

Introduction

1. hummingbirds will enthusiastically pollinate pineapple crops, which are native to South and Central America and the Caribbean, to the dismay of farmers.

Part I: Flights

1. American Bird Conservancy - Rufous Hummingbird Profile
2. American Bird Conservancy - Ruby Throated Hummingbird profile

1. Winter Holidays

1. Rico-Guevara, Rubega, Hurme, Dudley. 2019. Shifting Paradigms in the Mechanics of Nectar Extraction and Hummingbird Bill Morphology. Integrative Organismal Biology. Volume 1, Issue 1: pp 1-15.

3. Mating Season

1. Ars Technica. 2016. Bird brains are dense—with neurons.
2. Berkeley Rausser College of Natural resources. 2011. Hummingbird Tails Generate Sounds During Courtship.
3. https://www.macaulaylibrary.org/
4. https://www.fws.gov/laws/lawsdigest/migtrea.html

5. Raising a Family

1. Yanega and Rubega. 2004. Hummingbird jaw bends to aid insect capture. Nature. 428, 615.

www.ingramcontent.com/pod-product-compliance
Lightning Source LLC
Chambersburg PA
CBHW031151020426
42333CB00013B/617